The Peddler's Grandson

The Peddler's Grandson

Growing Up Jewish in Mississippi
Edward Cohen

University Press of Mississippi
Jackson

"Recollections of a Southern Jew." Selected portions reprinted from 1996 Smithsonian Folklife Festival program book. Used with permission of the Smithsonian Institution Center for Folklife & Cultural Studies.

http://www.upress.state.ms.us

Manufactured in the United States of America

02 01 00 99   4 3 2 1

The paper in this book meets the guidelines for permanence and durability of the Committee on Production Guidelines for Book Longevity of the Council on Library Resources.

Library of Congress Cataloging-in-Publication Data

Cohen, Edward, 1948–
    The peddler's grandson : growing up Jewish in Mississippi / Edward Cohen.
        p. cm.
    ISBN 1-57806-167-9 (cloth : alk. paper)
    1. Cohen, Edward, 1948–   . 2. Jews—Mississippi—Jackson—Biography. 3. Jackson (Miss.)—Biography. I. Title.
F349.J13C64   1999
976.2'51004924'0092—dc21
    [B]   99-10146
                                                                   CIP

British Library Cataloging-in-Publication Data available

For Kathy, wife, editor, best friend

Contents

Introduction

Back in sixth grade in Mississippi, I read a chilling tale, "The Man Without a Country," about a man condemned to live forever adrift on a ship, never to come home to his native land. My schoolmates, I imagine, took comfort in knowing that they were still on the shore and always would be. But I, being both southern and Jewish, identified with the man who had no home.

The Protestant South I grew up in was more like a Bible Blanket than a Bible Belt, not so much constricting as smothering everyone in commonality. Fitting in is the First Commandment of childhood, and for no one does this seem more imperative than for a child who can't. Of the hundred thousand people then living in my hometown of Jackson, perhaps three hundred were Jews, and so, by faith and by numbers, I was defined as an outsider. My life would have been far different had my immigrant grandparents stayed with other Jews in the North instead of inexplicably extending their journey even farther, to a land where Jews were as few as they were exotic.

As a child, I sensed that my family moved between two overlapping but impermeable worlds. There was the Jewish world inside the house, where I listened to and mostly understood my grandparents' wildly assorted mixture of English and Yiddish. And there was the world without, the southern world, which soon cloaked me like another skin and became a second self.

From the beginning, my life was intertwined with the Christian institutions that pervaded southern culture. I was born in Jackson's Baptist Hospital, attended an Episcopal kindergarten, graduated from a Baptist law school, served on a board of a Methodist college, and was married once in a Baptist Church and once by an Episcopalian priest.

Yet I was always aware of the vast divide between southerners and Jews, at the center of which stood Jesus, whom the overwhelming majority of the population accepted as their savior, while my faith accepted him not at all.

Beyond this chasm lay cultural differences, less defined, more confusing. Traditionally southerners had an abiding sense of place, revered the past, were chary of outsiders; Jews had been outsiders throughout history and had left all they knew behind when they crossed the ocean. Southern culture emphasized the physical—sports, hunting, at times violence; Jewish tradition exalted the mind.

Two powerful symbols of my divided identity stood at opposite ends of Capitol Street, the main thoroughfare of Jackson's downtown. At one end was the Old Capitol, built in 1832 with slave labor, the place from which Jefferson Davis proclaimed secession from the Union. At the other end was Cohen Brothers, the clothing store my grandfather and great-uncle founded when they came over from Romania, where my father worked all his life and where I worked every Saturday for much of my childhood.

When I was growing up in the 1950s and 1960s, Jackson was a Deep South capital where strangers waved as they drove by, said hello as they passed on the sun-warmed sidewalks. Jackson may have lacked the charm of river towns such as Greenville and Natchez, whose antebellum homes had been spared Grant's torch, but there were three weeks in spring when the air was not yet dense with heat and the azaleas flamed pink and red and magenta. Then my hometown was touched with the perfection that only childhood memory can impart.

I also recall that Jackson was a conservative town in every sense of the word. Political, social, and racial orthodoxy was ensured by the presence of the segregationist state legislature, by the Vatican-like power of the sprawling First Baptist Church, and by the hegemony of the city's sole newspaper, the *Clarion-Ledger*. The Junior League thrived there, a sort of grown-up sorority for young wives who were wealthy or could remember when their family had been, who were white, and who weren't Jewish.

The Jackson of my childhood was utterly segregated by race, with most blacks living west of downtown, poor whites mainly in the midcity, and most middle-class (and above) whites in the then-outlying northeast section of the city. It was there that all of Jackson's Jews lived and where our sole Jewish institution, Temple Beth Israel, was located, next door to the state Women's Club, which didn't allow Jews, and down the street from my high school, Murrah, which did allow Jews but not blacks. Farther north was the Jackson Country Club, which allowed neither.

Fortunately for me, the boy without a country, Jackson harbored pockets of liberal thinkers and other outcasts, and they, too, had their institutions, though much smaller and more fragile. Millsaps College was thought to encourage heterodoxy, and its graduates were suspect, unlike those turned out by the state schools such as Ole Miss. The state's public television affiliate, Mississippi ETV, where I later worked as a writer, was deemed a hotbed of communism and was forbidden by the legislature to broadcast *Sesame Street* because it depicted black children and white children playing together. Here and there were artists, writers like Eudora Welty, solitary messengers in the magnolia wasteland.

It was among these messengers that I would find myself most comfortable. From an early age I'd known I wanted to write. For someone adrift not only from the land of my birth but also from the moorings of Jewish culture, the calling came naturally.

One can hardly hail from two more historically losing causes than the South and Judaism. Both my cultures have long, tragic pasts, and not one jot of it has been forgotten. If my Jewishness and my southernness meant that I would have no home, no resting spot, I would at least have a singular view of the shore.

The Peddler's Grandson

The Big House

I saw all four of my grandparents together only once, in the early 1950s, standing on my parents' front lawn on a summer day, the two men proud of their American short-sleeved shirts. They conversed in English, though they would've been more comfortable speaking Yiddish. They came from countries thousands of miles apart, yet had a shared history about which they would almost never talk.

For my grandparents, time seemed to start at Ellis Island when they entered America as immigrants. Before that event was a great divide, and in their new homes were few family treasures passed down for generations such as those that graced the houses of their southern neighbors. There had been no room in their suitcases, so they had brought almost nothing with them, nothing to reconstruct their lost world except for a handful of photographs and fragments of stories that could only hint at what was left behind.

3

> *Schticky! Der kinderlach!*
> Southernized Yiddishism, meaning roughly "Little pitchers have big ears."
>
> "Peace at any price."
> My grandmother

My father's father, Moise (a variant of "Moses," pronounced "Mo-eeze"), walked to every hamlet and farm in Hinds County, Mississippi, with a pack on his back, peddling. The country folk took to the newcomer, a genial man who liked a good time and never corrected them when they southernized his name to Morris. He slept in their haylofts at first, and then, when they knew him, in their houses. For many, it was the first time they had ever seen a Jew.

Had Moise been more lettered in Jewish traditions and more observant of them, he would not have fit in so well. He would have refused the ham and greens the hospitable folk offered him, and they would have sensed that he was holding himself apart from them. But he did neither. Compared to Romania, where he'd come from, Mississippi was the Promised Land.

Romania, a poor, backward country, had been wholly untouched by the winds of the Enlightenment or any subsequent awakenings that had swept through western Europe only to stop dead at the Carpathians. Moise and his family lived in Vaslui, one of the tiny, rural villages known as shtetls that dotted Romania and all of eastern Europe. Directly across the river was Russia, and the Russian soldiers had grown accustomed to rock-throwing battles with the small, red-headed Romanian Jew.

Life in Vaslui was primitive, with mud streets and unpainted houses; not much had changed in the preceding three hundred years. Outside of business, Jews in Vaslui had little contact with Christians there. Moise's father, a cobbler whose name is lost to history, might repair a farmer's boots in exchange for a chicken for Sabbath dinner. Otherwise, Christians and Jews remained strangers to each other.

When my grandfather left Romania in 1889 at age fifteen, his departure was already overdue, for his battles with the authorities had not been limited to the Russian side of the river. Knowing he would never see his parents again, he boarded a cattle car packed with other immigrants and rode across the whole of central Europe to arrive finally at the seaport of Hamburg, his gateway to America.

In Vaslui, Moise had been known as a *wilde* (wild one), and Hamburg was famous for its red-light district. That night my grandfather was rolled for his passage money in a whorehouse. When the next morning dawned, Moise's ship sailed without him.

He could have gone home, might have been tempted to, but the pull of America was too strong, that and the dread of explaining why he'd come back. He was a proud man—those rocks he'd thrown at the Russian soldiers had been his reply to anti-Semitic taunts—so he worked for a year in a Hamburg cigar factory reearning his passage money, and then set out, not below deck in steerage but as a regular passenger with a cabin, as my father still likes to point out a hundred years later.

When Moise arrived at Ellis Island for immigration processing, he told them his name: "Kahane." Perhaps the immigration official craved uniformity, or maybe he didn't know how to spell what Moise said, but with the stroke of a pen, he changed the name to "Cohen," of which "Kahane" is a variant. My grandfather didn't protest; "Cohen" sounded more American.

Moise continued his journey another fifteen hundred miles to Mississippi for a simple reason—to join his older brother, Isaac Lazar. The other, more mysterious question, of how Isaac Lazar got to Mississippi, is unanswerable. Most immigrant Jews stayed in New York or in the Northeast near other Jews, but Isaac Lazar had inexplicably gone south to make his way in a world of Christians. He might have heard that a living could be made, or perhaps he wasn't used to, comfortable in, a totally Jewish world. Romania was not a center of Jewish learning. It was a hinterland, like Mississippi.

A few letters were sent back and forth between parents and sons, but the gulf between worlds was too great, and soon the letters ceased. Nor did my great-grandparents survive in the form of remembrances told to my father and then to me. Except for rare unguarded shards of stories, Moise's entire Old World experience was virtually obliterated. The old life was so bad and the new one so overwhelming that it was as if the Atlantic Ocean had washed my grandfather's memory clean.

It was a disjunction from past and family that would have horrified the southerners to whom Moise peddled soap and sheets and candy. Though my grandfather came from a tradition in which family was equally central, there were to be no southern-style reunions, not until a generation or two could replenish what had been lost when almost every living relative had been left behind. As for a Cohen family tree, what records there might have been were lost along with that entire branch of the family that didn't escape Europe in time.

In the late 1890s, a yellow fever epidemic swept through Jackson. As trains passed through the city with their doors and windows boarded shut to avoid contagion, Moise lay sick in one room of a nearby boardinghouse while Isaac Lazar lay dying in the next. When Moise recovered, he was alone. Uneducated and able to speak little English, he was in a place much farther from home than Hamburg.

Back in Romania, Moise's parents had one son left, Sam, and the Romanian king was drafting soldiers for an impending war. For Jews, the king's army was even worse than civilian life, since there was no escape from the anti-Semites in the barracks or on the battlefield. Moise sent money for Sam's passage, and, in 1898, Sam slipped out of the country, dressed as a woman to avoid the king's conscriptors, to join Moise in Mississippi.

When Sam stepped off the train in Jackson, the first thing Moise did was take him to a barbershop to have his moustache shaved off. Moise must have been adamant, since Sam obviously cherished his moustache enough for it to have survived his perilous escape from Romania when he was dressed as a woman.

Moise was not a philosophical man, but from his earliest days in Mississippi he seemed to grasp that to survive, to prosper, to be liked in a place where he was the first Jew most people had ever seen, he would need to assume some of the contours of his new countrymen. Inside, Moise was always a Jew, but his standards for remaining a Jew were not exacting. He set the family standard for assimilation.

Although Jackson at the close of the nineteenth century numbered only ten thousand, it was a grand metropolis compared with Vaslui. Horses and buggies plied Capitol Street to the busy hub of the city, the train station. Across the street was the plush Edwards House (later King Edward Hotel), where legislators repaired to rest and drink after their rigors at the capitol. Though much larger than Vaslui, Jackson had far fewer Jews—no more than fifty. But Moise wouldn't have come to Mississippi if he had needed an all-Jewish world.

When Moise was fairly "fresh off the boat," in his genial way he struck up friendships with some of the rednecks (as my father described them) who regularly reposed on the steps of the Edwards House. Though separated from Moise by an ocean of differences in religion and background, they shared with him a fondness for a shot of whiskey and the turn of a card.

He went with them out into the country, past the farms where he had peddled, to bet on cockfights, which were then common in Mississippi. Cockfights were about as far from tradition as a Jew might veer, but my grandfather was ecumenical in his associations. Had he stayed in New York and been surrounded by Jews, he'd have been perfectly happy with them, too, as long as they weren't particular about breaking the Sabbath if work or play required.

When Moise's cockfighting buddies proposed a snipe hunt, he naively and enthusiastically agreed. They took him to the grounds of the New Capitol, where the Mississippi legislature met, an area still thickly wooded since the building had only recently supplanted the state insane asylum. They gave Moise a bag, and, as the sun set, instructed him to wait high in an oak tree. They would fan through the woods, beating the ground and driving the mythological snipe up into Moise's oak, where he would bag them.

To Moise, snipe hunting sounded at least as exciting as cockfighting and was a sign he was being accepted by the Capitol Street layabouts. As it grew darker and much colder, my grandfather waited. He knew how to wait—hadn't he spent a year in Hamburg rolling cigars to reearn his passage money to America? It was very late, after many quickenings of the heart and readyings of the bag, when he slowly began to suspect the truth and clambered down, not feeling angry or discriminated against but rather the opposite, that he had undergone some redneck rite of passage and was more American for the experience. My father summed it up: "He was as green as goose *sheis* [gooseshit]."

Moise fell in with an unlikely group of Jewish peddlers who had made their way from Alsace-Lorraine to Mississippi. The pairing was odd, because Jews from western Europe typically were disdainful of the more newly arrived, less-educated eastern European Jews. Like the Alsatians, Moise walked every road of Hinds County, Mississippi, with a fifty-pound pack on his back, selling everything from coffee to bootlaces. When he ran out of goods, he rode the train to New Orleans to restock from wholesale jobbers, then took to the road again. On Saturday night, he'd rest his feet, drink whiskey with the Alsation peddlers and play poker all night, usually losing.

Moise and Sam saved enough money to open a small clothing store in Ridgeland, a town a few miles north of Jackson, where Sam sold dry goods while Moise continued to peddle. They had been there only a week when they received visitors, unsmiling men who hadn't come to shop but to deliver a clear, hard message: Jews weren't welcome. To Uncle Sam, newly arrived, it must have felt like he'd never left Romania.

They loaded their stock, moved back to Jackson, and opened a store in a prime location at 224 West Capitol Street, directly across from the Edwards House, near the barbershop where Sam had sacrificed his moustache to look American.

The anti-Semitism that Moise and Sam encountered in Jackson was less overt than in Ridgeland. When they entered an archery contest at the state fair and Sam the greenhorn remarkably won a horse, my father, then ten, heard the jokingly envious congratulations Moise and Sam received from their Christian friends. Then the congratulations went on too long and changed into something more telling. Fictionalizing, the gentiles recounted how Moise and Sam had held a raffle, and all the trusting Christians bought tickets. When the drawing came and they asked, "Who won?", Moise was said to have replied, slyly, "My brother Sam, that lucky dog." Everyone would laugh, but there was something else there that my father could see, in Moise's and Sam's forced smiles, in the gentiles' eyes that weren't laughing. "This is what Jews are really like" was the story's subtext, clear even to a child.

From the beginning, the store had an almost entirely black clientele. Moise and Sam had no credit and couldn't get the brand names carried by more established stores. What the immigrants could get was the merchandise that black customers could afford. It was an early example of the sometimes uneasy linkage between Jews and blacks who shared something neither wanted—exclusion.

For several years in the early 1920s, a time of fevered antiforeign sentiment, Moise and Sam told people they were from New York, not Romania. The Ku Klux Klan, with an antiblack, anti-Semitic agenda, made a national resurgence, and in Jackson held a huge parade on Capitol Street. They massed at the train station and then, in full-sheeted regalia, their faces hooded, marched past Cohen Brothers and proceeded to the Old Capitol at the end of the street, to the balcony where Jefferson Davis had, within memory of some of them, proclaimed the dissolution of the Union.

Moise stood in front of the store watching the parade, with my father on his shoulders. Moise pointed out one, then another of the masked marchers, some of them civic leaders, all thinking they were anonymous, and whispered to my father each of their names. The snipe hunters, the Edwards House layabouts, the jokers who had teased him about the archery contest—Moise recognized almost every one from the shoes he'd sold them.

My father's mother, Etta Cohn (she hardly had to change her name when she married), always maintained she had emigrated from England, to differentiate herself from the hordes of uneducated Russian and eastern European Jewish immigrants—like her future husband, Moise. The truth was she had probably acquired the pedigree from her brief stop there, en route herself from some abysmal village in Russia.

She came over with her parents and was securely settled in Rochester, New York, among thousands of Jews. Her father, Gershon Cohn, a tall stately man with a beard and, as my father put it, "not two nickels to rub together," sold yarmulkes (religious skullcaps) door to door. Kosher butchers could be found on every block and synagogues in seemingly every other storefront. Everyone around them spoke Yiddish.

Yet forces were at work that would dislodge Etta from this comfortably Jewish world. Her sister Ida, for reasons now lost, had married a salesman named Ike Levy, and Ike Levy lived in Memphis.

Uncle Ike was a travelling suit salesman assigned by the company up north to the godforsaken netherworlds of Arkansas and Mississippi. He drove a wagon pulled by two mules, necessary for the muddy bypasses between trees that were referred to as roads. The wagon was loaded with wool swatches from which stores from El Dorado, Arkansas, to

Meridian, Mississippi, would order suits. One of the stores in his territory was Cohen Brothers.

When Uncle Ike went out on the road, it would be for weeks, even months, at a time, so Ida sent for Etta to help with her two young children. Etta packed enough clothes for several weeks and set out, with misgivings, for the American South.

As Uncle Ike spread out his swatches on the long oak table in Cohen Brothers, he saw in the enterprising twenty-five-year-old Moise a good match for his sister-in-law. True, Moise was a frequenter of the *knafka*-houses in the red-light district a few blocks from the store—apparently the only lesson Hamburg had taught him was to watch his wallet. Yet he was also a young Jew well aware from his peddling days of the paucity of marriageable—that is, Jewish—young women; to marry a Christian would have been unthinkable.

After locking up the store at its usual Saturday-night closing time, midnight, Moise rose early Sunday to voyage to Memphis to meet Etta. What he saw was a small, formidable woman, tending just a bit to stoutness, with a lively sense of humor. She knew what was best for everyone, was right much of the time, and had a talent for accomplishing her many agendas, including taming the *wilde*, Moise. They were married in December 1908, not more than a few weeks after they met, beginning a pattern of short courtships and long marriages that would continue throughout the Cohen family.

Etta took the train back down to Jackson, permanently, and her younger sister, Nell, tall, slender, quietly elegant, came unsuspecting down to Memphis to replace her at the task of keeping Ida company.

Nell was unaware that Moise, perhaps at Etta's behest, had alerted Sam to her arrival. Soon, like Moise before him, Sam took the train to Memphis, and not four months after Moise and Etta's wedding, Nell boarded the train to Jackson to marry Sam. There were no more Cohn sisters to keep Aunt Ida company in Memphis. Moise and Sam's days of poker playing, not to mention Moise's visits to the *knafka*-houses, were over.

The two Cohen families moved into one house, insulation from the surrounding Christian world. The arrangement would continue for the next fifty years. In 1910, Nell and Sam had a son, Lazar, the first American-born member of the family. Moise and Sam managed to come up with two hundred dollars for a plot of land on Fortification Street, a couple of miles from downtown, and built a large house for the two couples and the coming children. In 1912, both sisters were pregnant at the same time, Etta with my father, Leonard, and Nell with Bernard (soon southernized to Buddy). A few years later, there was another double pregnancy when Etta had my Aunt Pearle, the only girl in the family, and Nell gave birth to Marvin, last born and forever known as Peewee. Because two brothers had married two sisters, Leonard and Pearle were double first cousins to Lazar, Buddy, and Marvin, an odd propinquity that would tightly bind that entire Cohen generation together for the rest of their lives.

Moise and Sam worked together all day while Etta and Nell kept house and reared the children. Raising two sets of children in one house created constant and novel issues of parental jurisdiction. Lines of authority fluctuated. Parents had primary responsibility for their children, but the other Cohen adults were a constant in-loco-parentis factor, which made it extraordinarily difficult to get away with anything.

The inevitable conflicts among the five children and four parents must've made the house a miniature Balkans. My grandmother's often-repeated motto—"peace at any price"—revealed the constant compromises that were necessary. Etta, whose nickname was "the General," ruled the house with edicts cannily leavened with cajolery, quelling a million tiny mutinies—complaints that she was "tight with the food money," that Pearle was pampered, or that Sam wouldn't let Leonard use the car for a crucial date—and if she didn't always suppress the insurrections, at least she quieted them in time for Shabbas, the Sabbath.

Every Friday night, after lighting the traditional Sabbath candles, Etta and Nell would serve redfish courtbouillon, a Cajun dish. No one saw anything anomalous about the pairing. Moise would allow the boys a shot of rye whiskey, which he referred to as his version of the kiddush, the Sabbath wine blessing. Etta's yarmulke-selling father would have thought his daughter had married into a family of peasant barbarians. Another of Etta's maxims was "It's a great life, if you don't weaken," and I imagine that the shock of the South was one of the earlier tests of her strength.

Excepting the Sabbath, virtually every other night of the week featured chicken from Etta's backyard coop, the birds killed and plucked while the children watched the carnage from upstairs, so that once my father left the Big House he never ate chicken again. As for Moise, he preferred catfish, which fed on the river bottom and was utterly *treif,* forbidden under kosher dietary laws. When he was single, Moise had liked to go to New Orleans to eat fried catfish and drink whiskey, or he'd travel to Vicksburg to catch catfish himself in the Mississippi River. Etta wouldn't eat it, wouldn't even cook the fiercely ugly whiskered thing, and sometimes must have wondered what sort of Jewish goy she had married.

At all mealtimes, Moise had one firm rule: once the doors of Cohen Brothers were locked, no talk of business was allowed until those doors were unlocked the next day. The urge to talk about a matter so vital to both families must have been overwhelming, especially after Lazar and my father reached their teens and helped out in the store.

Moise's requirement that business never be discussed outside the store was part of a larger attitude. Because of the tight quarters and intersecting lines of authority, certain hypocrisies were essential for survival. Discord was never acknowledged. When anger was expressed, it was punished, regretted, apologized for, and most of all denied. The mythology, as I heard it growing up, was that life inside 730 East Fortification Street was a Jewish heaven of peace and laughter. The Cohens, at least on the surface, lost their characteristic Jewish bluntness, and this newfound tact helped them blend in with their Christian neighbors.

For the Cohens who grew up in a double family in the Big House, as the story was passed down in family folklore, life was a sort of southern-Jewish Huck Finn existence. Lazar, the eldest son, had the broad shoulders of a swimmer and enviably thick dark hair. He and my father were more like brothers than cousins, even double first cousins, and they'd bolt from Sunday school to play with their friends, all Christian. The temple, like most of the town, was near the railroad tracks, and soot would blow from passing trains through the open windows, blackening the faces of the small congregation. All the Cohen boys joined the Boy Scouts, attended the YMCA's Camp Kickapoo, and in the summer swam in muddy Livingston Lake.

At night, the boys slept on a screened-in sleeping porch, seeking relief from the fabled Mississippi heat. Pearle, the sole female and princess of the family, had her own bedroom with a mahogany bed. This position of privilege endowed Pearle with an illusory reputation of wealth throughout her life, and she was sometimes referred to in the Jewish community as "the heiress."

More than once, during Prohibition, all nine Cohens were awakened by loud bangs emanating from the basement. My father and Lazar, still in high school, had brewed homemade beer with Moise's help and capped it too tightly. In contrast to their Baptist neighbors, who were teetotallers, they had set up an entire brewery, including a capping machine, in the basement. Their Christian neighbors would've been horrified and prayed for their lost souls.

Moise and Sam traded Sam's horse in on their first car, an Overland, to carry the double Cohen family to Rochester to meet their northern relatives. Upon arrival, and every day thereafter, their grandfather Gershon sent Leonard and Lazar with an empty bucket to the corner brewery to fill it with beer, which they always sampled before turning it over to the learned yarmulke salesman.

Suddenly the Cohens were in a world that was urban and Jewish. These relatives were faster talking and faster moving; they seemed faster thinking. They argued. The Mississippi Cohens—the phrase seemed an oxymoron—were already set apart after two or three decades in the South.

The Rochester visit came not many years after the well-publicized case of Leo Frank, an Atlanta Jew accused of child molestation and lynched when the demagogues inflamed Atlanta with anti-Semitism. The Rochester cousins wondered what sort of violent wilderness Etta and Nell had cast themselves into. Was the South any different from their native Russia? The family was frightened for them.

Yet by this time Etta and Nell felt that Jackson and the South were home. Jews lived in China and India—why not Mississippi? Moise and Sam had their daily ambit from Fortification Street to Capitol Street, where one of the rich German Jews, Mr. Dreyfuss, daily walked his pet duck in front of the governor's mansion. To buy merchandise, they borrowed money from a Christian at a bank, reversing the stereotype, and did business with that family for the rest of their lives, a pattern followed by the next two Cohen generations.

Back on Fortification Street, in the Big House (as they all called it, unaware that this was the name for the old plantation mansions), Etta and Nell raised the double family. They fed the backyard chickens and shared accented pleasantries with the Christian neighbors, trading Jewish recipes for southern. Though they were very different from their neighbors, they made every effort to fit in.

The younger generation mirrored that effort. Leonard and Lazar, who would end up lifelong business partners, mixed easily with the Christian boys in the neighborhood. My father, recollecting, described himself as a "Jewish redneck." But he also recalled frequent taunts of "Jew-baby" and equally frequent fights to settle the matter. In contrast to their northern cousins, Leonard and Lazar were not averse to settling matters physically, like the southerners they were becoming.

The process of southernization was abruptly halted when it came to dating. Etta had yet another credo: "Marry your own kind." Unlike the other Cohen boys, my father was a *wilde*, as Moise had been. Leonard was drawn to Christian girls, and Etta envisioned each casual date as a potential shiksa daughter-in-law. Etta ended romance after romance, a Jewish Cerberus zealously guarding the gates of her tradition. After a forbidden date, my father would take elaborate precautions—parking far down the block, taking off his shoes, tiptoeing up the stairs—and at the top she'd be waiting, a never-sleeping protector of the faith. She would easily deflect his initial protestations of innocence, thread her way through his torturously textured stories, and finally after a lengthy interrogation pluck out from him the name of the shiksa. The poor girl, if she called, would be told to stay out of the Promised Land. As my father later complained, "It took time and money to get something going and I had to start all over."

My father kept Etta vigilant and worried for many years; he didn't marry until he was thirty-four, after he had come home from World War II. But her teaching had taken root, and he, like the four other Cohen children, married within the faith.

All the children remained close by in Jackson. When the old folks moved to a smaller house, the possibility of the two couples' splitting up was not even discussed. The Big House was unoccupied, another overlarge early twentieth-century house in an increasingly commercial area. By this time the children were managing the old folks' affairs, and they tried without success to sell it. Then a plan was conceived that would bring life and the Cohens back to Fortification Street. Someone in the Jewish community had passed along a blue-print for a four-story apartment complex that would fit per-fectly on the Cohen acre. Two of the Cohen families would live there, each occupying a floor, with the other two floors rented out. The fact that this obviously doomed plan was even a consideration is a testament to the powers the Big House, even in decline, held for the Cohens it had shel-tered. The plan fell apart. The new generation of Cohens, first to be born in America and in the South, were more comfortable extending themselves farther into the encom-passing gentile world.

I was nine when my father took me for my only visit to the Big House, by then long uninhabited. In the back was a fig tree, ancient and overgrown, its limbs reaching through a broken basement window, starting nature's slow reclama-tion.

The rooms of the house seemed too small to have held all the people and stories. My father showed me the closet where Aunt Pearle at age five had saved her double first cousin Marvin from a mouse, resulting by unclear etymol-ogy in Marvin's nickname, Peewee. The mouse closet was dusty, moldy with the Mississippi damp, but as my father told the story I could strip back the interceding decades and visualize the epochal event, as I did in the decaying base-ment that had been the Cohen speakeasy. When he showed me Moise and Etta's bedroom, I felt as though I were looking upon the chambers of some ancient semimythological regents. I stepped into the shower with the circular curtain that had wrapped itself around them like a wet anaconda. My father, always cautious, wouldn't let me step out onto the fabled sleeping porch.

The house stood empty until it was sold to the Baptist Hospital, where all of my generation of Cohens had been born. The bulldozers took it down in a day. The monster fig tree planted when the century was young was torn from the earth. The sleeping porch tumbled to the ground. When I drove by, I wished incongruously that the fig tree could have been somehow preserved. But then I would have liked for it all to have been saved, every shard representing memories of a past now distant and increasingly unrecollected.

Soon the raw earth was paved over and all that was left of the Big House was a dip in the curb where the old driveway had been, where daily for half a century Moise and Sam had returned together from the store to Etta and Nell and their double families, their Promised Land of milk and honey and redfish courtbouillon in the midst of the Christian wilderness.

Whereas my father's people came over from Romania, my mother's parents had come from Poland, and that made all the difference. Poland was a horribly backward place, as described by my mother's parents, but compared to Romania it was positively cosmopolitan. Poland had several Jewish centers of learning, even if my grandfather's little shtetl wasn't one of them, and Jewish learning and lore were inescapable. But Romania. Moise's shtetl, Vaslui, was an almost feudal place. Its Jews were more rural and isolated, and across the ocean this translated to a tendency toward ignorance of Jewish lore and a great deal more comfort with the ways of the South.

I know much less of my mother's parents than of my father's, partly because they lived four hours away in Shreveport, Louisiana, but mainly because they died when I was so young. I have an ancient photograph of my mother's father, Ben Weltman, taken, as the delicate scrolled engraving on the picture announces, in Krakow, Poland. My grandfather, a tailor by trade, was dressed finely. Like my Uncle Sam in Romania, Ben had fled to America to avoid the army, though much later, in 1913. He'd had several brothers, but he was the only one to immigrate, so very likely they all perished in the Holocaust.

Ben had the same fine features as my mother, as well as her eyes (and mine), at once combative and too sensitive. When I look at that eastern European photograph, one of the few artifacts that made the journey with him from Poland to the American South, I see the eyes of an exile and in them an early shadow of sadness.

After being in this country for forty years, he was still far from any place he could call home. As he lay in the Baptist Hospital in Jackson, Mississippi, with leukemia tracking his veins and arteries, he said to my father, "You work all your life to pay the doctor and the undertaker." Something of his dark view was passed on to my mother and through her to me. The placid joviality of Moise would've been a more comfortable temperament, but Moise would never have been driven to write, or even to reflect overmuch on the day's business.

Ben, whom I called Tottie in my child's rendition of the Yiddish "tante" for "father," was not placid. My mother confessed one day that Tottie could be described as a socialist, or, based on the Yiddish-language newspapers he subscribed to, a communist. My father, with his southern horror of any deviance from the norm, insisted it could not have been true.

My grandmother Rae is in another one of the fine Krakow photographs, she, too, finding it hard to raise a smile, though perhaps it was just a fleeting sadness or a reflection of the general tenor of life for a Jew in Poland. She had a gentle face, and I remember most a feeling of warmth and comfort from her even as she was dying, as she was for almost all of the few years I knew her.

Growing up, I'd always heard the stories of Moise's immigration, his audacity, his perseverance, his unwavering pursuit of America and of being American and southern. Only later did I hear of my mother's relatives, the more ambivalent ones, the ones who wanted to go back, and I immediately felt a kinship with them, much more so than with Moise's intrepid cheerful adaptability.

Ben and Rae had initially settled in Buffalo, New York, but Rae, pregnant with her first child and lonely for all that had been familiar, begged Ben to return to Poland, the known evil infinitely preferable to the incomprehensible. Instead, they moved south to Texarkana, where she had a friend, then on to Shreveport. Rae for the rest of her short life never adjusted to America. Her English remained poor, and she never became a citizen. So terrified was she of the new land that when she took Ben his lunch every day at his tailor shop she packed all her silver and took it with her. Once when the family crossed the border into Mexico for a day jaunt, she became terribly fearful that she wouldn't be allowed to reenter. Even more than my mother, Rae was an internally displaced person. While Moise had strapped on a pack and stuck out his hand to the new land, Rae lived inside, where she embraced longing and memory.

Rae's parents embraced it with her. Rae's father, my great-grandfather, had left Poland for America with the dream of earning enough money to send for his wife still in the old country. When his ship docked in New York, no one was there to meet him. Perhaps there had been a miscommunication or a delay, but all he knew as he looked out on the teeming dock was that he was alone. He immediately went back to Poland into the arms of his disbelieving wife. As soon as he returned home, he knew he'd made a terrible mistake and tried to come back to America, but by that time World War I had erupted and he was trapped.

Finally, he and his wife made it back to America, where they joined Rae and Ben in Shreveport and moved into the house next door. A photo of them, taken in what must have been 1930, shows a bewildered couple from another world and time. Their children had chosen to venture southward and they'd been too old not to follow.

By installing Rae's parents next door, Tottie and Rae created a tiny Jewish center in the north Louisiana hinterland, and drew Rae's four brothers there. My mother, Pauline, small even for seven, with her eyes in photos showing both sharp intelligence and already that inexplicable sadness, was assigned the duty of teaching English to her four Yiddish-speaking immigrant uncles. Every day they would walk up and down the streets of Shreveport, the four adult Jews, still in their dark eastern European suits, bent over to receive instruction in English from their tiny niece, listening to her as diligently as if she were some sage rabbi. I don't know what pedagogical method Pauline, obviously untrained at age seven, employed to teach them a whole new language and alphabet, but it worked, and in later years as they spread out from Shreveport through Texas and up to Kansas City, they spoke a heavily accented but perfectly sound English.

As for Pauline, who'd given up her play time for family duty, the lesson was plain—life is work and work must be done, always. In due time she passed this Jewish work ethic down to me, where it warred with the easygoing relaxed southern approach—"philosophy" would be too grand a term—that Moise took to naturally.

My mother's upbringing was more Jewish than my

father's and not only because of their parents' country of origin. Nor was her training due to any intense religious feeling from her parents—not with Tottie reading those socialist/communist newspapers; it was simply the result of a Jewish presence in Shreveport larger than the one in Jackson. Numbers provided a buffer against southern assimilation. The photo of her temple confirmation class depicts a group of perhaps fifteen teenagers, each representing a Jewish family and providing a strand that could create a semblance, an illusion, of a Jewish world in this southern isolation. By contrast, my father's confirmation class photo shows four thin boys, gathered around their rabbi, like the rear guard of some decimated and besieged army making a hopeless last stand. With no one around to reflect and reinforce tradition, memory had to be lost and with it large chunks of identity.

Unlike my father, my mother never was at home in her native South. She did not suffer gladly anything done slowly, circuitously, or sugar sweetly. She was a woman of the 1990s born fifty years too soon and two thousand miles too far south. When she married my father and moved farther south to Jackson, she said it was "out of the frying pan and into the fire."

When Pauline was in college, she suffered a romantic heartbreak. I learned of it only after she was dead, from her oldest and, in the end, perhaps her only friend, her brother's wife, my aunt Marcia. Aunt Marcia never lost her Brooklyn accent even after decades of living in the various southern towns to which Uncle Louie's oil business exiled them. Aunt Marcia also never lost her northern directness and her acerbic pragmatism; in this, she was very like my mother.

My mother, a small, dark-haired beauty with delicate, sharp features, had been very bright in school and had skipped two grades, so when she went off to college she was only sixteen.

The University of Texas in Austin was a huge campus that would have swallowed almost anyone up. My mother, who had grown up in a household where no one ever hugged, kissed, or remembered birthdays, put on a brave exterior as she stepped into the world, but her armor was fragile. She met a Jewish boy from Texas. That is all I know, except that Aunt Marcia referred to him as "the bad penny" because for years he kept turning up in my mother's life.

Either in person, or through his never-sleeping proxy, memory, he followed her when she abruptly left Texas and transferred to the University of Illinois; he then pursued her into the WAVES, the women's naval corps, which she had joined after graduating and returning to Shreveport and finding that it seemed very small.

It was while she was in the WAVES that she discovered New York City and found for the first time a place that felt like home. New York held glamor, sophistication, an intellectual life—all the things that excited her, that she'd never seen in the South.

World War II ended, and my mother returned from Manhattan to Shreveport. She was now twenty-eight, which in 1946 was considered very old for a woman to remain unmarried. She'd had numerous proposals, refusing them all. If there had been little for her in Shreveport before, there was nothing now, and she made her plans to leave the South and emigrate to New York.

Then fate, the hunter, reached out, in the form of a letter from Aunt Marcia. Uncle Louie had been transferred to Jackson, Mississippi. There Aunt Marcia had become friends with cousin Lazar's wife, Lolita Stein Cohen.

Lolita was a person about whom no one could remain indifferent. She was warm, dynamic, controlling, always at the center of some emotional storm. She could make even the most banal gossip interesting, at least for the moment when it was lit by the incandescence of her focus. She was a small stout woman who fought her weight with the same fierce dynamism that attended everything she did—mounting shopping safaris to little-known jewelry wholesalers, undertaking exotic travel, outfitting her home so that it was a suburban museum of good taste. Her consuming passion, however, was for arranging lives. It gave her an almost artistic satisfaction, and she was a master at it.

Lolita had married Lazar, but there were three more Cohen boys returning to Fortification Street from World War II, not to mention all the other needy Jewish bachelors in Jackson. After hearing from Aunt Marcia that Pauline was beautiful, single, and Jewish, Lolita immediately lined up seven suitors for my mother, who, unaware in Shreveport, was packing for New York. The visit to Jackson was to be only a temporary diversion, a comfortable visit with her sister-in-law before she stormed the northern ramparts.

The first date Lolita arranged for my mother was with Lazar's youngest brother, Marvin. Next she went out with Buddy, and they made plans to see each other again. Then came my father's turn in Lolita's roster. Afterward, he went back to the Big House and announced that Pauline was his.

One month to the day later they eloped. They left Aunt Marcia's house, drove forty miles to Vicksburg, Mississippi, and were married by the rabbi in the small temple there. My mother wore a purple wool suit with a purple wool hat, and the temperature that late October day was over ninety degrees.

Why did they elope? My father was a dashing figure, known as a bit of a rogue (he had inherited Moise's uncomplicated enjoyment of a good time), but once he had seen the most beautiful girl to come into the tiny Jackson pool of eligible Jewish women, he would not let her go. Perhaps my father's passionate tenacity showed my mother that she would always be loved and made her as eager as he. Their love affair continued until the end of her life.

They took several honeymoons—first to the Robert E. Lee Hotel in Jackson right after the wedding, then later to Biloxi on the Gulf Coast, then to Havana (and a cockfight). On one honeymoon, she wrote that she had never believed she could be so happy. For the rest of her life she would live in Jackson.

Her transition into the Big House and the world of the Cohens was not an easy one. She refused the wifely duty of taking Etta from one grocery store to another, from the Jitney Jungle to the A & P to another Jitney Jungle in search of the lowest prices. "I'll be happy to take your mother to *one* grocery store," she said to my father, who was caught between two difficult women, "but not two or three and not every day." My father placated her and Etta, and the charge remained with Etta's daughter, Pearle.

My mother cherished ideas but had no one to discuss them with. Had she lived in the North, she could have been a part of the tradition of Jewish intellectualism there. Had she been a Christian, she would have found a larger reservoir of seekers after knowledge. In many ways she had traded life for love.

My father, ever loyal, would dutifully listen as she sometimes didactically, and often with no concept of the level of interest of her audience, would present some new philosophical, scientific, or artistic concept she had gleaned from her constant eclectic reading, which ranged from Ovid (she had been a Latin major) to the *Encyclopedia Judaica*. "Life is a play with a badly written last act," she might note to him, by way of Cicero, or, from George Eliot, "It is never too late to be what you might have been."

The moment she had finished and he had come up with a gallant display of appreciation, he would return to the newspaper, television or, more likely, some private worry whose depths he was sounding.

I would like to be able to say that I joined with my mother in her intellectual passions, that I encouraged her when she tried to share her life of the mind. But I did not. I wanted to find my own way, and I saw her conversations as lectures, long pent-up monologues. Once, when Ralph Salomon, my Jewish best friend, came by to visit, she trapped him at the breakfast room table for close to an hour. He listened as courteously as my father but said to me later, "Doesn't anyone ever talk to her?"

No one did, not really. She was not an easy person to talk to. She was so easily wounded that she never guessed that she herself could wound, that her sharp tongue kept almost anyone from coming near. She was never aware of the effect on others of her piercing appraisals, never perceived that in the South, among women, even among Jewish women, views were not expressed unvarnished. In a rare moment of opening herself, she said to me that if she could have one thing in all the world, it would be an understanding heart.

Almost never can I remember her sharing a personal distress. She had the highest tolerance for pain, physical and emotional, that I have ever witnessed. When she had acute glaucoma, in which pressure builds and builds behind the eyeball, producing what most would consider unendurable pain, my father and I were utterly unaware of her condition until even she determined it could be borne no longer. She had waited so long that her sight was permanently damaged.

Because she never complained, she suffered the isolation that came from never speaking about her feelings, from rejecting the support that might have come from giving up a little piece of her secret self in exchange for some succor. As I grew older, she had fewer and fewer friends, until finally there were none, so she went where people would need her. She was a faithful volunteer at the Baptist Hospital where I was born and at ETV where I worked.

Mostly, she withdrew to a private world of learning, to the public library, a welcoming place that she visited several days a week, returning home with a canvas "Jackson Metropolitan Library" bag full of poetry and observations on all aspects on life. Montaigne, de Tocqueville, Byron, Goethe, Catullus, Marx, Freud, Darwin, Auden—all found their way to Brook Drive.

There, she would immure herself in a chair in the den, all day, late into the night, surrounded and protected by a moat of books, notebooks, and a manual typewriter. She'd rummage through the volumes, unearth quotations that spoke to her, type them by author, and file them in one of ten gigantic overstuffed binder notebooks. From this would come her "Pearls of Pauline," a weekly one-page selection of epigrams, many of which she disagreed with, all selected to pique curiosity or make people think. She had a subscription list (free) of around twenty-five people. If people would not listen to her, perhaps they would read her "Pearls." Perhaps they would comment on one of her quotations. And sometimes, someone would.

When I was three, my mother took me from Jackson to live in Shreveport while she cared for her mother, Rae, who was gravely ill. I saw my father only on weekends, when he'd drive the four hours to be with us; my mother would cry when he arrived and again when he left. With my mother distracted and my father appearing, then mysteriously disappearing, every week, my only steady link with what I knew as home was our maid, Gladys, who had made the trip with us, leaving behind her own family. The unnameable terrors of my inexplicable exile were soothed by Gladys's soft, black, southern voice, and in its unexacting curves and crevices I found a refuge and a semblance of my lost home.

By contrast, my mother's voice was brisk, with no nonsense in her vowels, which got the job done and moved on to the next syllable. She was Jewish, which meant that sentimentality was a luxury she couldn't afford, particularly then. Her voice was bracing, and I was reassured by its clarity that there was nothing in the shadows. Her voice was also sharp, though certainly more so because she was caring for a dying mother, a stunned father (who was even then himself mortally afflicted though no one knew it), and for an exceedingly sensitive child who wordlessly absorbed their grief.

At last, my mother and Gladys and I came home, bringing my grandmother to live for the remainder of her days in the ranch-style home that my parents had just built. The duty to care for her had fallen naturally to my mother, from age seven the assumer of duties.

Tottie stayed on alone in the little house in Shreveport and went off every day to his tailor shop, a thin figure with a few friends, all Jewish, someone who spoke with an accent, unknown and unknowable to his southern neighbors, none of whose traditions he had adopted. His mind was elsewhere, in the world described by those flame-like Hebrew characters in the Yiddish newspapers, and his heart was 250 miles east, fading away in our suburban American home.

One day at his tailor shop a robber knocked him unconscious with a soft-drink bottle, stealing the meagre amount he'd rung up that day. The doctors remarked it was fortunate that the weapon had been a Seven-Up bottle, because a heavier Coca-Cola bottle would've instantly killed him. It was while he was being treated for this wound that the doctors discovered he had leukemia. Soon he gave up his little store, and my mother traveled to Shreveport to close up the house she had grown up in. She kept only a few items of furniture, disposing of the rest unsentimentally and returning to Jackson with my grandfather.

He moved into our guest room with Rae, sleeping now

in suburban twin beds. As they spent their final time with us, I felt a sorrow that was distinct from my personal grief. Tottie and Rae, who had not taken easily to the South, seemed in some way to be my link with my Jewishness. Every day as they diminished more, I mourned what I know now to be a passing away of the source of my Jewish self. Tottie, in particular, with his worldly-wise but uncynical eyes, his gentle, sad, understanding smile, was taking with him my history. Soon, a year later perhaps, they were both gone, buried in the Cohen plot at Beth Israel cemetery on North State Street in Jackson, the first to go there though they weren't even Cohens, for they had no place else to go.

My mother remained to embody for me the old Jewish ways, but they were diluted, like all traditions. Besides, like her free-thinking father, she wasn't religious, believing that the Bible was composed of instructive stories written not by God but by men inspired, perhaps, by God. Religion was not what made a Jew a Jew, of that she was certain, as certain as she was that her Jewishness was the core of her being. Much of that Jewishness, I gathered, was defined by the Christian world. It derived, in roughly equal measure, from how you guarded yourself against the Christian world and how that world, in turn, set you apart.

Worlds in Collision

"In the name of Jesus Christ, our Lord. Amen."
Conclusion of the daily school prayer broadcast over the public address system

"Why weren't you in school yesterday?"
Fellow first grader, after one of the Jewish High Holydays

When I was growing up, it was a point of civic pride that Jackson was "the buckle on the Bible Belt." Christian churches were everywhere, and, naturally, so were Christians, a multitudinous army compared to our tiny camp. Yet until I was six, I lived sheltered from that South in an almost entirely Jewish universe, with little premonition of the cultural clash that would await me when I started school.

What made my home an all-Jewish universe was the simple fact that, with very few exceptions, no one who was not Jewish ever set foot inside it. Such an insular existence would not be odd, would even be the norm, in places such as Queens or Israel where almost everyone was Jewish. What was remarkable was that, in Jackson, my parents and the majority of other members of the Jewish community drew exclusively from their tiny group of three hundred fellow Jews to form their circle of intimates.

The innermost sphere was the extended Cohen family. The five Cohen families produced numerous children, and these double cousins enforced my childhood illusion that the world, at least insofar as that world had any real significance, was made up entirely of Jews, primarily Cohens.

The families were close, if not always in affection then certainly in familial duties to the patriarchs and matriarchs, Moise and Sam, Etta and Nell. The old folks had moved into a smaller edifice on a pleasant tree-lined street, Windermere Terrace, the site every Sunday afternoon for my entire childhood of the weekly gathering of the Cohens in a much-expanded reconstitution of the Big House.

To Christians, Sundays meant church, then lunch together at some family site or perhaps at Morrison's Cafeteria. For us, Sunday's primary significance, apart from the fact that it was the sole day the store was closed, was the weekly conclave, which began at one o'clock and lasted at least until five.

Attendance was mandatory. It was as if, in the absence of a large Jewish community to support our identity and sustain us in the midst of the surrounding thousands and millions of Christians, we pressed every member of the family, from age three to eighty, into service to do the job.

As a result, the knots of my relationships with the other Cohens were complex. We were bonded together centripetally by exclusion from the outside and by the family's unvoiced but unquestioned assumption that the highest allegiance was owed to family, more than to America, to the South, perhaps even to Judaism.

Because of our double-blood relationship and two-family background, the cousins my age who gathered on Sundays had a special kinship, more than mere attenuated cousindom. I was especially close to Lazar's son, Gary (we worked together every Saturday at the store) and to Pearle's daughter, my first cousin Roslyn, a small sturdy girl with dark bangs and credulous eyes that hid a wickedly twisted satiric mind.

While the adults were discussing canasta and children— Moise's moratorium against store talk was still in place, though he and Sam had retired—Roslyn and I would hone our imitations of popular schoolmates, with Roslyn portraying the head cheerleader while I was the captain of the football team. Our imaginations would transport us to church, to student council meetings conducted with utmost Christian politeness, to awards ceremonies for the Daughters of the American Revolution, to the crowning of Most Christian Boy and Girl, and to the venues of their unfathomable dates, where we would be, half-mockingly, half-yearningly, Normal-for-a-Day.

Back in the den, Moise would be sharing a shot or two of Scotch with Lazar, my mother would be attempting small talk and waiting for five o'clock, my father would be itching to talk about the store, Lolita would be cross-pollinating the news of the other hundred-odd Jewish families, and Granny would be locked in intense colloquy with her daughter, my aunt Pearle.

Absences from the weekly Cohen summit required copious excuses. Nonattendance was allowed for illness, which would be discussed at some length. Two successive weeks' absence for this reason caused concern; we were few and could not afford to lose any of the soldiers in our army of identity. Simple desire not to go to Granny's, which my mother expressed on more than a few occasions, was insufficient. In the end she always went, because duty to our family and to the larger Jewish family prevailed over individual preferences. Thus were we inoculated with an intense concentration of family and Jewishness for the coming week.

From Sundays at Granny's I learned that a Jewish house was a safe house. There were two other Jewish homes on Brook Drive, the Dormans' and the Oppenheims', and I sensed that they were secure places, whereas the others seemed somehow threatening. Scattered throughout Jackson were other Jewish households, like little islands of safety in a menacing sea, and I'd be taken to one or another, hopscotching from welcome to welcome, not ever wondering why I never visited the other houses.

The only Christian homes I entered in my early childhood were our next-door neighbors', the Lefoldts on one side, the Millers on the other. I could tell that my parents were comfortable with them. They mourned the death of my first pet, a toy Manchester named Tony, and my second, of the same breed and name. I had permanent permission to visit the Millers and their many cats, and to coast on my bike down the Lefoldts' driveway, under the low pine branches, to make a precise landing in my parents' carport. In those innocent times, the Lefoldts had all the neighborhood children over every Halloween to bob for apples, and I felt as comfortable in their benign domain as I did at Cousin Lolita's or Aunt Pearle's.

As to all the other Christian houses, it seemed safer not to enter them. I did have Christian playmates in our neighborhood, such as the son of the Methodist minister whose church was only a few doors down the street. During the time the minister's son and I built a go-cart, we must've spent every allowable hour together, but we always met on neutral territory—the street, the yard, the elementary school playground. By contrast I was in and out of the Dorman house several times a day.

Whereas Christian men gathered with others of their kind for hunting and fishing or bowling, and their wives joined social clubs with names like La Petite Fortnightly, for Jews card games were the social glue, the matzo meal, that bound them together.

From the time I was able to remember, my mother played canasta almost every afternoon of the week. It was the Hebraic version of a sewing circle. The game rotated from house to house, with two, sometimes three tables set up, each with five to six players. Thousands of miles from New York, my mother and her canasta friends were manning their unlikely outpost of Jewish civilization.

Women from Beth Israel streamed in and out of my house. Those canasta ladies remain mythological figures to me, gossiping and kibbitzing and smoking cigarettes in the living room as I peeked in. Our maid would serve coffee and sandwiches, which the women would consume without taking a break from the talking and cardplaying and always the smoking. My mother would circulate through the room from time to time with a silver silent butler, emptying into it, like the ashes from a biblical sacrificial offering, the charred butts from three hands and four stories previous.

In a central position in the room was the large and matriarchal Eva Sussman, the acknowledged queen of Jackson Jewish gossip. With only a hundred families to supply material, artistry and imagination and a never-silent phone were essential to keep the stream of conversation replenished. Nearby would be my cousin Lolita, and, at the second table, or the third, would be Aunt Pearle, who also worked, reluctantly, at the store on rare breaks from canasta. In the same room were Granny, Aunt Nell, all my other female relatives in Jackson, and the rest of the cardplayers, who were somehow almost relatives.

Matters of substance were not discussed. There was no debate over whether Israel posed a threat to Jewish assimilation or the advisability of getting a bomb shelter, no discussion of Senator McCarthy's fulminations or of Governor Faubus and Little Rock. The talk was more likely to be about the latest offense by our impolitic rabbi, Perry E. Nussbaum, or about food, Jewish food in the hinterlands. They might get several minutes' worth of conversation, at multiple tables, about the introduction of a so-called Jewish rye bread at the Jitney Jungle. The bread was made locally by bakers who, as my grandmother would say, knew *bupkes* (beans) about Jewish rye bread, and in truth it was a virtually tasteless beige bread that bore as little resemblance to the genuine article as would the concoction of a Brooklyn rabbi's wife who might improbably try her hand at corn bread.

Jewish staples such as real rye bread and kosher salami and gefilte fish were precious and would remain unobtainable until 1961, when the Olde Tyme Delicatessen opened. Until that time, Jackson Jews, like Russians in the gulag, had to rely on care packages from relatives up north. When one arrived, it was a time of celebration, differing not in kind but only in degree from when manna had been sent by another Jewish relative. The salamis and rye breads would be apportioned among the Cohens, not always in a wholly equitable manner, and there were loaves that might have been skimmed off the top in a weak moment. If we Cohens went anywhere outside the South, we took an extra suitcase so we could stock up for the lean months, as our forebear Joseph had taught the Egyptians to do. It was our way of keeping the faith.

As I made my pass through the card room, I was enveloped in a bath of smoke and smiles and kisses. Then the next day, my mother would be gone, to Flo's or Leota's or Phyllis's, for another round. There was something enormously reassuring, even nurturing, about those canasta games, seeing those same faces every week for years in my living room, or knowing that the identical faces would be gathered nearby in another Jewish home.

At night, returning from their daily commerce with the Christian world, Jewish men would gather at the house. The game was poker, not every night because they, unlike the women, had to work, selling clothes or watches or insurance. I would peek more fearfully at these deep-voiced, gruff members of the male southern Jewish world. Unlike the women, who played for *pishkes* (nominal amounts), the men played for real money, and the room was forbiddingly serious. There was little cigarette smoke. Here it was cigars, and the room was thick with haze and Yiddish curses. Our formal, rarely entered dining room—otherwise used only for Thanksgiving dinners and Passover seders—was transformed into an intense field of manly competition, both frightening and awe inspiring to me at age eight. Southern Christian men played cards, too, but they had other channels for their competitiveness and aggression—football and hunting. Poker, a game of survival through wits, was the natural and sole field of combat for the Southern Jewish men I knew.

In contrast to my mother's card games, which I was allowed to watch, uncomprehending but fascinated, from my seat on the sofa, the men's play I could witness only briefly from the adjacent breakfast room. Among those ringed around the dining room table might be Lazar (Lolita was just a few feet away in the living room) and Pearle's husband, my uncle Melvin. Uncle Melvin was a hearty, gregarious man with a shock of black hair, a perennial short cigar, and a big hard belly that he allowed me to punch as hard as I could (until his heart attack).

The cardplayers who at temple tousled my hair now stared right past me. The most important one, the only important one, was my father. He was tall, carrying a little extra weight but still handsome, a bear-like man with kind eyes and also a temper which, on the few occasions when he lost it, caused him great remorse. In all my other dealings with him, he was solicitous, ever sympathetic to any worry or grief I might have.

This gentler side of him seemed to vanish when he stepped into that smoky poker area. I didn't dare approach him, his cigar firmly clamped in the corner of his mouth, his whiskey virtually untouched, his pile of chips growing. So on poker nights, I waited, in the breakfast room or in my room, on the chance that he would take a break and let me know everything was okay. And he always would.

He was an excellent gambler and at one point had considered becoming a professional. That he'd even contemplated such a precarious—and wholly un-Jewish—livelihood hinted at the impossible contradictions his personality contained. He was frequently impulsive and utterly daring— riding the cards at the blackjack table in Las Vegas (and, it seemed, always winning), expanding the store, eloping with my mother. In this he was Moise's son.

Yet paradoxically—and this must have come from Etta—there was a constant governor on his spirit, a curb of caution that sensed danger everywhere. In our family, my father was the Jewish mother. Whether it came solely from Etta or from being Jewish in a sea of Southern Baptists, he was extraordinarily protective—in contrast to my mother, who was from the no-nonsense school of child rearing. When I was a toddler and my parents were going out for an evening of dancing on the Heidelberg Hotel roof downtown, I would cry and he would come back inside, torn, until my mother, with a sharp note in her voice, informed him, accurately, that I would stop once he left. He worried the whole time and called the sitter throughout the night. He still has the unread copy of a book my mother gave him, Dale Carnegie's *How to Stop Worrying and Start Living.*

My father instilled in me a pervasive fear of lockjaw and other diseases. Every childhood scratch convened a family council to conduct a two-part inquiry: "Did it break the skin?" and "Was the nail rusty?" My father always carried the day, and before the sun had set—we were unsure how long we had, and I was already opening and shutting my jaw for creaking sounds—we'd be at Dr. Meloan's for a tetanus shot.

My father also taught me, through example, to check closets in the house more than once a night to see if anyone was in there; to look in the back seat of the car before entering; to shake the locked door upon exiting a home or store, then go back at least once but more often twice to reshake it; and to fear any dog larger than a cat. These habits did not always serve me well when later I entered the Christian world.

On a few occasions in my early childhood, Christians did enter the house, as for a mixed (Jewish and gentile) ladies' poker game. Its origins lay in the limited cross-cultural camaraderie found at the Colonial Country Club, which, unlike the elite Jackson Country Club, allowed Jews and to which virtually every Jewish family in Jackson belonged. These games were much more formal than the canasta-klatches, and I sensed my mother was not at ease, brittle, as if the slightest disagreement would shatter the unnatural union.

The Christians were different from the Jewish ladies, more restrained, polite, with very sweet smiles, soft voices, and pretty blonde hair. The talk was not the freewheeling, animated bazaar of gossip that accompanied the normal games—after all, what did these ladies care about rye bread?—so my mother and her friends molded their tones and topics to meld with the visitors. Yiddish expressions were suppressed, with great difficulty and not always successfully. The weather was explored exhaustively, while the commentary on the game was more genteel, as if winning were unimportant. None of the Jewish ladies wanted to seem too "Jewish." They were on their Sunday-school-best behavior.

My mother, normally an indifferent housekeeper, would have scoured the house and taken great care with the food preparations—nothing too spicy, not even a hint of garlic. An equal amount of planning was required for the seating arrangements—no clumps of Christians in one area, no Jewish ghetto table.

Of the two groups, the Christian ladies seemed more comfortable; after this dip into exoticism, once they stepped back outside they would again be swimming in their amniotic southern Christian universe. As they glanced around the house—carefully, not wishing to seem nosy—they might have noticed the odd little mezuzah on the door, the Hanukkah menorah in the breakfront, the plates on the wall depicting the story of the exodus from Egypt, the absence of their usual sausage ball hors d'oeuvres and green punch.

Absorbing my mother's unease, I was vaguely uncomfort-

able at the presence of the courteous outsiders, who constituted additional disturbing evidence that the world was not
an entirely Jewish, or safe, place.

This fact was traumatically confirmed on my first day of
school. I was an only child, the first male in the family,
greatly cherished and protected by my parents and grandparents, cushioned by the matrix of four other Cohen families living nearby and by the larger network of other Jewish
households in Jackson. When I walked the fifty yards from
my backyard to the front door of Boyd Elementary School,
I found that I was crossing over into a foreign land populated by those unsettling people who, until now, I had
thought were the exception to the homogeneous Jewish
norm.

Looking around my class, I felt overwhelmed, just as any
child would on his first exposure to the huge jostling
world—a room full of strange faces, our parents gone, the
lady behind the desk telling us to raise our hands if we had
to go the bathroom, and, most of all, incomprehension as
to why we were there. For me this was compounded by an
engulfing feeling of surprise and displacement.

Looking at the teacher and at my twenty-nine classmates,
I saw that the world was not constituted of Jews. I'm not
certain *how* I knew they weren't Jewish. At age six, could I
have perceived that the girls in the class had fairer, softer
features and looked like miniature versions of the visiting
gentile card ladies? Or was it my classmates' singsong
drawls? Though my parents had southern accents, all my
family had been raised with relatives whose raw immigrant
accents diluted our drawls, cutting through them like a
shock of clear astringent turpentine through thick gummy
paint.

Whatever the answer, I knew that my class was populated,
dominated, by an entirely different species. I was the only
Jew in my classroom, and at lunch I saw perhaps five or six

others scattered like flecks of sand throughout the other grades in the school of five hundred white Christian students. (In 1954, the year I started school and the year of the Supreme Court's school desegregation decision, there were no blacks at any of the white public schools in Jackson, nor would there be for another decade. I was thus utterly insulated from any racial or ethnic heterogeneity, except, of course, my own.)

As I tried to find a seat in the cafeteria, carrying my tray of overcooked, overfried, and (to me, then and now) inedible southern food, I vaguely recognized the older children I'd seen at Friday night services and at Sunday school. At temple they'd seemed big, powerful. At Boyd they looked dwarfed. I pushed the food around on my plate so it would look like I'd made some inroads into the viscous string beans and gray meat. I noticed that the other children around me were consuming their lunches with no apparent cultural displacement.

Back in the classroom, where puny electric fans batted hopelessly at the September heat, I looked from my desk across the street to my house and saw every detail of my lost world . . . our black maid hanging up sheets that lay limp, baking in the breezeless day . . . my mother, driving to the grocery, back from the grocery, to her canasta game . . . the giant air-conditioning unit, pumping ceaselessly. I yearned to be there.

When the bell rang at 2:15 and children spilled from Boyd Elementary School, I waited until the sixth-grade Safety Patrol boy let me pass, ran across the Lefoldts' yard, and crossed the border into my yard with joy and relief.

School, as a one-day experiment, had been tolerable, excepting the cafeteria. I had seen the world and I was ready to return forever to the familiar, familial, Jewish world that had been mine for the last five years.

The next morning when my mother ruthlessly packed

me off to school again, I thought of the older children there, and the still-older children at the larger high schools, and suddenly realized that my life had somehow forever changed. Some force even larger than my parents was compelling them, and me, to the outer world. My father felt my distress. Although he might not have understood the workings of my as-yet undiagnosed artistic temperament, he, too, had once been cast out from a Jewish Eden to be the only Jew in his class. If there had been a way to keep me at home forever, he'd have found it. Building a house just across the street from my future school had been the next best thing.

On the second day of school, and on the days that followed, I felt a continuing disquietude, but it was almost a month before my forebodings took a concrete form, with the arrival of the Jewish High Holydays, Rosh Hashanah and Yom Kippur. Though religious observance in my family was inconstant at best, my father always closed Cohen Brothers, taping up a hand-lettered sign, "Closed for Religious Holiday."

Before I started school, the coming of the High Holydays meant only that I had to go to temple for what seemed an endless and incomprehensible service, after which I'd be set free to play. Now that I was enrolled in school, I had to receive permission from the officials of the larger world, and my mother wrote me a note to take to my teacher.

Mrs. McPherson was a kindly person with a bun of gray hair, but she had a sharp tone in her voice whenever the class got unruly, a tone not dissimilar to my mother's, and I was terrified of her. More importantly, I did not want to call attention to myself, did not want to appear—or be— different. In my one month's experience in school I had never seen anyone take a note to the teacher and had no idea of the protocol or my chances of success. I wished that I didn't have to take the note up there; no one else had to.

What if, somehow, magically, the note and the holiday were to be lifted from me? It was the first time I realized how much easier everything would be if I weren't Jewish.

I waited all day for a good moment to deliver the note, which by that time I had furtively folded and unfolded, read and reread, pocketed and repocketed, numerous times. My mother's crisp vertical handwriting, I felt, might as well have been the flagrantly foreign Hebrew letters of my tiny scrolled child's Torah.

At the end of the day, when I couldn't delay any longer, when everyone was gone except two girls who apparently were never going to leave, I wordlessly handed the note to Mrs. McPherson. She read it and said, with a not-unfriendly smile, "Happy Rosh Hashanah, Edward." The two girls stopped talking and looked at me.

The next morning I stared out the den window at everyone normal going normally to school and suddenly found myself yearning to be there rather than be different. Wearing my little sport coat but, thank God, no yarmulke, I got in the car with my parents. My father, so it seemed, was the only grown man in Mississippi not at work.

At temple I saw my fellow Jewish classmates, themselves wrenched from Boyd. After the service, I was driven home, where I spent the day in my special spot on the roof of the house, staring across at Boyd, wondering what my classmates were saying about me. I hoped my mysterious absence had not been noted, or that it would be chalked up to some one-day malady. If I could just get through the next day without explaining, no one would know. I was forgetting, of course, the one-two punch of Yom Kippur at that moment swinging my way in just nine days.

When I returned to school, I was marked not only by my classmates' curiosity but, just as importantly, by how I felt about being different. I couldn't tell which was stronger, only that one acted upon the other, making me feel more and more separate from everyone around me. I assumed a tiny burden of otherness, one that would grow through the years as it shaped me.

One classmate, a loud blond boy, approached me as I sat in my desk before class, attempting invisibility.

"Why weren't you in school yesterday?" he demanded.

I knew that classmates who had been sick weren't challenged upon their return, not even the girl who had been out for the dreaded and highly contagious pinkeye. Nor were the ones who, not daring to raise their hand to go to the restroom, had drastically overestimated the absorptive capacity of their underwear and had to be mopped-up after and sent home to change clothes. These trangressions, it would seem, were subjects far more worthy of inquiry than my little absence.

Children do have an instinct, and my interlocutor was only voicing what the rest of the class was sensing.

"It was a holiday."

"*We* didn't get a holiday."

"A Jewish holiday," I mumbled. In truth, that was all I knew about it.

Now there was genuine curiosity from him, as well as from the others who gathered.

"What did you do?"

"Just went up on my roof," I said, eliding over the long morning at Beth Israel.

His inquiry was cut short by Mrs. McPherson's call to order. The group dispersed, all but my classmate, who looked at me even more oddly.

"Went up on the roof?"

I struggled for words, but he was gone. It was too late. In trying to downplay my difference, I had only enhanced it. He now believed that Jews spent religious holidays on top of their houses, a far more weird and exotic ritual than praying in a house of worship.

The second High Holyday, Yom Kippur, approached, unstoppable. Again, I took the note to Mrs. McPherson. Again, everyone watched me and heard her sincere if inappropriate "Happy Yom Kippur" (on the Day of Atonement, Jews review their failings of the past year). The next morning I again put on my sport coat while everyone else was streaming to Boyd in jeans and T-shirts. At temple, I sat between my parents, back in my all-Jewish world, which, now that I had tasted of the apple of otherness, no longer felt as secure and encompassing. My conception of reality was stretching, painfully and daily, to embrace a gigantic new Christian and southern universe.

After the short children's service, my mother took me home. I stripped off my sport coat and shiny black shoes and threw on my school clothes so I would look normal. I would have loved to have gone on the roof but was scared someone across the street at Boyd would see me and think I was atoning.

The next day at school, I hoped I wouldn't be asked about my second suspicious absence. No one said a word about it. They didn't need to.

Before I ever stepped across the street into Boyd school and the Christian world that hot September morning in 1954, everything I'd seen and been taught had etched a mark on me in invisible ink. All it took was exposure to the other world to make it legible.

I have proof in a photograph, taken when I was five and attending St. Andrew's Episcopal kindergarten, held in an old high-ceilinged house on a hill, the site subsequently occupied for many years by the YMCA and later by the First Baptist Church as a Christian health club. My Jewish bubble was still intact, probably because of the temporary nature of my attendance; I would spend only half a day there, after which my mother would whisk me back to Brook Drive.

My parents weren't concerned about my attending this Christian-affiliated kindergarten. Episcopalians were considered to be the most educated and tolerant of the Christians, and there were no prayers at St. Andrew's. Most important to my mother, however, was the fact that St. Andrew's was simply the best kindergarten, where drawing and French were taught; the paramount Jewish canon of education prevailed over any discomfort about sending her child to a school named after a saint.

In the photo of my class, seven of us are seated at tables, drawing, and behind us are two teachers, their hair neatly permed. Everyone is looking at the camera, as instructed— except me. I am determinedly, fixedly, looking down at my drawing. There is something willful about the stare of this small, blond, sensitive-looking boy. Like any child, I wanted to be the same, but simultaneously I raged against it.

My divided loyalties, my ethnic acrobatics to fit in while I remained apart, continued throughout my years at Boyd. In those days, every morning began with the teacher reciting a prayer, and every prayer ended with "In Jesus' name." The prayers, particularly the ending, made me feel sacrilegious, disloyal to my parents and Tottie and to myself. We Jews didn't believe in Jesus, didn't believe he was the son of God, though I knew by this time that everybody else did. I thought about not bowing my head so I wouldn't be participating. I tried not closing my eyes but I still heard the prayer. It was just three words, "In Jesus' name," but they were inestimably important, to my classmates in their acceptance of them, to me in my rejection of what everyone else believed. I never even considered protesting. I was a child, one who knew better than most the First Commandment of childhood.

When I was ten, the teacher announced that there would be a Christmas pageant and asked who wanted to participate. I looked around at my classmates, their raised hands waving like the banners of Crusader regiments. They had no conflicting feelings. I felt again the weight of otherness. We didn't celebrate Christmas for the same reason we didn't say "In Jesus' name." Christmas seemed not only alien but dangerous, and staying apart from it was in some way integral to my very identity.

I stared down at my desk, studying its carvings and stains with ferocious attention. I was very aware of Christmas because of my father's clothing store, where the holiday season was the busiest time of the year. There, unlike at our home, Christmas decorations (safely secular images of Santa and his reindeer) went up. Christmas gifts of candy were given out to regular customers, though the customers' greetings of "Merry Christmas" were returned with the more neutral "Happy holidays."

I watched Miss Holderfield copy down the Christian children's names for the pageant. I recalled the year I had begged my mother for a Christmas tree. It had seemed like a fun and harmless thing, with all the presents under it and the lights and decorations. In those days, when every house and every neighborhood was lit up in festive solidarity, our home couldn't have been more conspicuously dark than if, like the Israelites in Egypt, we had daubed blood over our doors.

My mother refused, at first patiently, defusing my argument about the store's decoration by simply ignoring it. We had Hanukkah, a minor military holiday transformed by the combined pressure from thousands of Jewish children over the years into a substitute Christmas, with a present each night for the eight nights we lit candles. But I wanted a tree.

Exasperated finally, she said it would have to be in my room with the door shut because she wouldn't have any Christmas tree in her window. It was characteristic of her that she didn't take the easier approach of some Jewish parents, who, without rabbinical sanction, were buying small, squat Christmas trees and renaming them Hanukkah bushes. They'd put a Star of David at the top and hang little figures of the Maccabee warriors and a few incongruous Santas for variety. To my mother, this was nothing more than an agronomical ruse. Anyway, a Hanukkah bush wasn't what I wanted.

I got a small artificial tree and set it up by myself in my room, placing some decorations my father had given me from the store on its green metal bristles. For the eight nights of Hanukkah, after my parents and I lit the candles in the menorah to celebrate the biblical miracle of the oil lantern continuing to burn in the temple, I shut myself in my room and plugged in my tree—the modern miracle of the Jewish Christmas tree. This solitary celebration, watching my single lonely strand of lights blinking, with my eight saved-up unopened Hanukkah presents underneath, was profoundly dispiriting. (My participation in Easter egg hunts, which my mother inexplicably allowed, was equally unsatisfying; I worried that at any moment I would be exposed as an impostor and forced to give back all my eggs.)

As Miss Holderfield's volunteer sheet for the pageant filled, I held back. That night, when I brought up the Christmas pageant to my parents, I had very mixed feelings. I dreaded being branded by my classmates as different, as on the High Holydays, but I also felt that participating in the pageant would be some kind of betrayal. The pageant, after all, was going to enact the birth of Jesus, and there was no getting around that with ecumenical Santas or so-called Hanukkah bushes.

My mother decided the issue much as she had the Christmas tree affair, with accommodation but without acquiescence. The ruling of the family Sanhedrin Jewish court was that I could not play Jesus or any of the major figures. I could work backstage, or, if absolutely necessary, I could play a rock or other inanimate object. I didn't know how to explain these fine casting differences to my teacher, so I opted for pulling the curtains, hidden, while onstage all the Jewish roles were played by Christians.

With such a small role, I spent most of the rehearsal time sitting forgotten in the empty auditorium, while onstage everyone else, students and teachers, were caught up in the spirit of something that eluded me. They were all members of a giant club from which I alone was excluded. Every Sunday the club's members went almost as one to churches and then afterward to Morrison's Cafeteria. They talked year-round of the unbearable excitement and yearning for Christmas Eve and of rising early to fall upon their presents like hungry wolf puppies. They sent and received Christmas cards (that sad substitute, Hanukkah cards, had not been invented). The club was extremely easy to enter. All I had to do was give up everything.

My parents attended the pageant, of course. I was their son, and having themselves been raised in the South, they knew of the compromises necessary. My mother smiled the way she did at the ecumenical canasta games, while my father was as proud of me pulling the curtain as he would have been if I had played Moses in a Passover pageant. I could see them from backstage, surrounded by the other parents, for whom attendance was not a minor act of apostasy. I opened and closed the curtains, participating but invisible, part of it but apart.

At the end when I took my bow with the Three Wise Men, the rock, the tree, and the rest, I was comforted to see my parents out there, smiling and clapping, as if we were just like everybody else.

In many ways I was. I dressed and looked and acted like any southern boy. I wore Keds sneakers with soles that quickly became as slick as a banana skin, unelasticized white socks that bunched around my ankles despite rubber bands, formless blue jeans with grass-stained knees patched with primitive 1950s iron-on patches that soon peeled at the corners, then fell off entirely. My blond hair was shaved up the back and high over the ears.

My mother was active in the PTA and I was proud to see her there fitting in. Her intellectual sensibilities were outraged when we switched from phonics to the more free-form word-recognition theory of reading, and she led the charge against it to vouchsafe her son's future. As encouragement, I received a quarter for every "High" on my report cards and double that for every "Very High," real money in those days, evidence of my father's generosity and my mother's determination that I learn everything. I delighted in guessing the homework that would be assigned and doing it in spare moments, so that when the teacher wrote it on the board and I was right, it was like seeing my horse cross the line.

During recess on Boyd's huge back grounds, I played softball and kickball, reaching my athletic apogee when for a brief time (until everyone else got taller) I was on the school basketball team. My greatest strength was stealing the ball mid-dribble from more long-legged opponents.

I grew accustomed to the Christian world. Exceeding the grudgingly expanded geographical limits that my father allowed, my friends and I rode our bikes to the newly conceived shopping centers to drink nickel cherry Cokes, up the Natchez Trace, and out past the city limits to explore creeks and swim in the then-unpolluted (or so I hoped) Pearl River. We took school trips to the Old Capitol Museum downtown to view with pleasant revulsion the genuine Egyptian mummy, which was later removed from display when a strip of the Memphis *Commercial Appeal* newspaper was discovered protruding from its bandages. All these experiences intensified my southern identity. For hours, even a day, it would not occur to me that I was anything other than a regular normal Mississippi boy growing up in the tranquil, unquestioning 1950s.

Then, every night at home, I was reencapsulated in a Jewish microcosm, and the only Christians I saw were on our big black-and-white TV. From my den window I could see the darkened, sleeping Boyd, where in the morning the Safety Patrol boys would, like border guards, wave me across the street into my alternate universe.

There we were ruled by the tough-but-just Miss Power, a fierce-faced, frizzy-haired bride of the Jackson Public School system, who bore an unsettling resemblance to *Have Gun, Will Travel*'s Richard Boone. Like all semimythological creatures, Miss Power had abilities that transcended the merely adult. She could appear anywhere the moment a child did or thought wrong, in any classroom, on the playground, on the farthest reaches of the Safety Patrol's jurisdiction several blocks away. Being sent to her office was like consignment to a dragon's den.

Yet the room that held the greatest terror for me was not Miss Power's office. It was the cafeteria. Proust had his madeleines; for me all it takes is the smell of frozen fish sticks frying to bring back the long tables filled with screaming children and a plate staring pitilessly up at me. Fish sticks were served every Friday, their thick fried breading not quite masking the swampy reek that would grab me by the throat ten feet from the cafeteria door. None of the other children had any difficulties with the fare, but for me the cafeteria was the site of my most profound clash with southern culture.

Unlike southerners, my mother did not derive her culinary heritage from the plantation. Her mother had taught her European Jewish dishes—kreplach, stuffed cabbage, potato latkes—and to these she added her own brand of eclectic American cooking. Though she hated cooking as she did all housework, my mother was nonetheless inventive in the kitchen. She did serve southern staples like collard greens and black-eyed peas, but they weren't rendered to mush by all-day stewing. Vegetables were always fresh, never greasy with salt pork, lard, or fatback. I never faced a Campbell's cream-of-mushroom-soup casserole, nor frozen salmon croquettes, nor white-grease gravy over chicken-fried steak. Greater by far was my terror of a teacher's forcing me to "clean my plate" of institutional southern cooking than of any subtle dilution of my Jewishness from Christmas pageants or Easter bunnies.

Sometimes I passed the teachers' inspections by desperately stacking my food to make it look smaller, wadding it in a paper napkin, or hiding it under the plate, from whence it would slowly and greasily leak over my tray. Some teachers, zealous and implacable, were not fooled and would stand behind me until I'd forced down enough to satisfy their standards of nutrition and obedience.

Then Dave the janitor would have to be summoned. Dave, like Miss Power, was an eternal figure of indeterminate age. He was a tall black man, grave and dignified even when rolling the metal vomit-mobile down the daily-buffed linoleum tiles to mop up some accident, then swab the area with uncut ammonia. The wet spot would remain, much enlarged from the original deposit, with the sharp antiseptic fumes wafting through the room and out into the halls, a sulphurous cautionary warning. Like fish sticks, ammonia is Proustian for me; all it takes is a sniff to bring back those gray-green cafeteria walls and the day of my forced ingestion of some fatbacked collards.

I wondered how Dave (that was what we all called him though his hair was going gray) felt in my white world and whom he talked to during the long work day. Once I saw him sneak a few words to one of the five black cafeteria workers. Otherwise he must have been totally silent for the eight, nine, ten hours he worked. My sole attempt to speak to him provoked intense awkwardness on both our parts and was never repeated.

Most of all, I wondered where he went to the bathroom since all the rest rooms were white. I learned, one day after school, when I went into a small back hallway. Signs didn't have to posted to let me know this excursion was not allowed. I had spotted Dave's room before, a narrow door at the end of the hallway. Dave, I knew, would be mopping the empty classrooms.

I turned the knob. Unlocked, as I expected. Somehow even at that age I surmised that a black man would not have a locked room. I stepped inside a very small, very neat room. There was the vomit-mobile, and his cleaning products, and an extra uniform hanging slumpshouldered from a bent wire hanger. This small room contained an even tinier room with a door. Inside was a toilet, his private segregated toilet for one.

Feeling I'd seen something somehow shameful, I hurried out, not wanting to be caught by a teacher but especially not by Dave, whose world of tenuous dignity I had invaded. I looked away the next day when I saw him in the hall, as if I had trespassed into more than a room.

The version of history that I absorbed both in the classroom and out was the same one in which my fellow southerners were steeped. There had been no civil war but a War Between the States, and, almost a century later, I, like my classmates, referred to northerners as "Yankees." When we sang "Dixie," we stood as if it were the national anthem. Visiting the battleground at Vicksburg, just forty miles away, I ventured into the imposing Union monuments and felt as if I were standing in enemy territory. In fiction and in fantasy, I rooted hopelessly for the South to win, and I cherished the *Look* magazine article about what would have happened if we had not lost.

Unlike virtually all my classmates, I couldn't trace my family history to antebellum plantation lords or to dirtscrabble farmers; my heritage only went back to Moise sleeping in their haylofts. My lack of lineage only increased my fervor. I wanted to embrace what could never, even in memory, be mine. There was something irresistibly bittersweet about the Lost Cause, about what might have been, how I might have belonged. The Confederacy was an anomaly, as I was.

It is a foolish, romantic affliction, historically foreclosed and politically every shade of wrong, but I still think of that day—my birthday, July 3—at Gettysburg and if only Lee had done it right. Being Jewish and being southern made me root doubly for the underdog.

No matter how I tried, I could never be southern, not wholly, a realization I had most clearly when I came in contact with "rednecks," rough working-class whites. Middle-class Christians held many of the same values my family did—education, tradition, manners—and as different as they were from us, they didn't seem hostile. Rednecks were more threatening, and their children carried with them an edge of violence. Some of them were my friends, my best friends. They lived in Broadmoor, a blue-collar subdivision just across Northside Drive from my house.

My Broadmoor friends spoke of being whipped with belts by their fathers. At first I didn't believe them, so alien was the image. In my family my mother occasionally administered a few swift swats with her stiffened hand, which, with a sharp word, were more than enough to bring tears, while my father waited in the other room for it to be over.

When I visited my friends' homes, the sense of dislocation that I'd always felt in any Christian dwelling was compounded by the poverty—yards of weeds and dirt, yellow-brown stained sinks, small rooms with too much furniture. The mothers always looked harried, worn out, and they treated me gingerly, as if I might break. The fathers (the ones I knew wielded the belts) treated me with a mixture of contempt and awe, contempt because I didn't know the meaning of a hard day's manual work, awe because I didn't have to.

I dreaded supper at my friends' houses. As at Boyd I couldn't eat the food, but here it was personal. I didn't want to insult my friends, be disrespectful to their mothers, anger their fathers. I tried to eat, but I could not cross that culinary barrier any more than if I'd been offered goat's eye in a herdsman's tent. One mother kept offering seconds when the first helping was substantially intact, and the father, proud, missing nothing, asked, "Not good enough for you?"

In the same neighborhood, when I was nine, I had a more traumatic encounter with that side of the southern world. Riding my bike home, I saw some classmates in an overgrown front yard and coasted into the driveway to visit, when suddenly a large black dog wheeled without warning and bit me in the calf, then as quickly slunk away. The boys continued playing as if nothing had happened, though I had several puncture wounds, each oozing blood. The dog had no tag.

Its owner, a large forbidding man in overalls and no shirt, emerged through the torn screen door of the house. I didn't want to cause trouble, but I knew rabies was fatal, and that the cure, intramuscular injections, was legendarily painful. In a quivering voice, I asked him if the dog had had his shots. The children, who I'd thought were my friends, banded together and told the man I had provoked the dog. Without a word of apology or explanation, the man went inside. I pedaled toward home, my pants ripped, leg bloody. The children, a living wall of hostility, watched me. I was scared. I knew I'd have to go back.

My father came straight home from the store and we

drove back to Broadmoor. The same kids were in the front yard—the dog was gone, to protect him—and they stared at me with undisguised dislike. If they'd been bitten, their parents wouldn't have cared, so why was my father there? They played, ignoring me, as I sat in the car. My father—at the time I didn't realize the courage this took—knocked on the door. With the car windows rolled up, I couldn't hear what they said to each other, but it was ugly, and I could see the man angrily gesturing, getting louder, then slamming the door. As we drove away, I could feel the children's hard stares. Thereafter, I avoided that street on my bike.

My father called the city, and the pound came for the dog and observed him for the requisite ten days. At Boyd, the dog owner's son and his friends formed a little clot of animosity whenever I chanced past them, even after the pound had returned the dog, now vaccinated. Somehow it was all my fault, the dog's being taken away, my justifiably concerned father, his insistence that the dog's angry owner, who was given to letting things slide, comply with the law. My father might not have faced down a mad dog the way Atticus Finch did in *To Kill a Mockingbird*, but to me he was every bit as brave.

> "Why don't you join the Women's Club?" I asked my mother as we drove by a stately brick building. I hoped she might belong to something.
> "No Jews allowed," she replied tartly.

As I grew older I found myself more and more confused about my place in the southern Christian world. Physically, until I was eleven, I could have passed for Christian. "He looks just like a *shaygitz*," my relatives would proudly exclaim every time they saw me. *Shaygitz* is Yiddish for a male gentile; as with the genderless "goy," the connotation is vaguely derogatory, solely because gentiles are not Jewish. It was enormously perplexing to me. Apparently, the ideal was to look like a Christian but in all other respects be Jewish.

My straight blond hair seemed an anomaly to me, for the original biblical Jews, from whom we descended, had dark hair and dark eyes. During their two-thousand-year diaspora into Europe, clearly a considerable number of Christians had dipped into the Jewish gene pool. Yet the origin of my father's blue eyes and Moise's red hair was never discussed. Intermarriage, in those days a sin against blood second only to conversion, was paradoxically both undeniable and unspeakable.

Intermarriage did not become a major factor in my life until the sixth grade, when invitations went out to my entire class to attend a dance class in one of the columned mansions on North State Street, where we would learn to rhumba, waltz, and samba. There would even be an introduction to a new dance, done to rock 'n' roll.

These last months of preteen years were the age when "liking girls" was still questionable and possibly temporary, with the boys in the class split evenly on the issue. Southern Jews not being known for forthrightness, I said I saw merit in both positions. In truth, the dance class was enticing, though I carefully kept any enthusiasm out of my voice as I allowed my parents to argue me into it.

The allure had curdled into terror by the night of the first class. Wearing my child's-size clip-on tie, I climbed into my parents' giant Olds. It felt as if I were stepping into the tumbrel that would carry me to the guillotine.

All the most popular girls in the school were there. However, all the most popular boys were, too. Partner selection was a harrowing Darwinian experience, as the most beautiful naturally paired off with their like and a scramble ensued at the lower end of the scale. I was never sure of my ranking. *Being* Jewish didn't have so much to do with it, I thought, as *looking* Jewish. By that time, my blond hair had darkened and curled, and I couldn't remember the last time anyone had said I looked like a *shaygitz*.

After twelve excruciating weeks, the dance maestro, a tautly strung man who carried about him the air that he had once lived in a much finer place and done better things, made an announcement. There would be a party, and boys would have to find a partner among the girls in the class. A date.

Every day in school I looked around the classroom at the girls, with the enthusiasm of someone selecting a suicide weapon. As far as I was concerned, there were no possible candidates. Some were too pretty, others were too popular. Many were already too tall. Still others I rejected with the same ruthless Darwinism my classmates exhibited. As for the remaining few, I chose to assume that they had already been asked, the likelihood of which increased with every day I delayed. My dim hope was that if I waited long enough all the girls would be taken.

My parents wouldn't grant me clemency. My father, showing a rare lack of empathy, couldn't comprehend why I would be terrified. He was as sociable as Moise had been and had enjoyed every moment of schooltime romance. My mother's grim position was that I had signed up for the class and I would have to finish it.

One morning at 8:29, as my classmates milled toward their desks, suddenly I was seized with initiative, and before my courage failed, I approached a girl I had vaguely considered possible.

The issue of religion never entered into my considerations. The world was a Christian world, I knew, and there were no Jewish candidates. I had never in my young life encountered any overt anti-Semitism, and I didn't then. By 8:30 I had a date. She was no doubt as relieved as I was.

In the days to follow we never spoke, though we did nod to each other in the hall in acknowledgment that some faint relationship had formed. Boyd was fairly egalitarian, and I had no idea of her family's social standing. The school district was mostly suburban middle-class white, though at one edge was Broadmoor, while at the other border was an enclave of genteel columned homes, with large swaths of lawns, private ponds, and regal moss-hung oaks planted when the owners' ancestors had arrived.

At the appointed hour, my parents drove up a long driveway to one of those columned homes. The two-story brick structure was imposing, starkly unadorned, somehow cold-looking. For the first time I realized my date was wealthy, but this discovery didn't alarm me since my terror was already complete.

I sat in back, costumed not only with my clip-on tie but in a striped sport coat my father had gotten wholesale through his haberdashery connections. My date's family was one of the wealthiest and most socially prominent in Jackson, mainstays of the First Baptist Church, a powerful, prestigious, and profoundly conservative organization. Her father was probably a deacon in the church, whatever that was. My wool pants, also gotten wholesale, itched.

Clutching my corsage, I stepped onto the columned porch and reached up for the large brass knocker. The girl's father opened the door and looked down at me. All I could take in was his very close-cropped hair as he silently let me inside his mansion.

I had been in rich Jewish homes in Jackson. They were modern, splashy with art from travels to New York and even Europe, but I hadn't been daunted. I saw the local Jewish upper class at temple, and some of them played cards with my parents. No matter how much money they had, they were citizens of my world.

Entering any Christian home, no matter how many times I had visited friends, was always an immersion into otherness, but this, the world of the Christian rich, was so different, so distant, that it somehow posed less of a threat. There was no chance of my being subsumed into this world.

I stood in a huge formal foyer, furnished with the kind of very old oak furniture that comes only through inheritance. The ceiling was so high I couldn't see it without losing my balance. In the very short time I was in the house, I never penetrated farther than three feet past the front door and never exchanged a word with the Deacon. My date, in a pastel dress stiff with petticoats, was immediately escorted in by her formally smiling mother. I was back outside in under a minute, into the Olds, listening to my mother assay a few courtesies to the girl in the tone I'd heard her use at the ecumenical canasta games. Soon, the car subsided into silence.

The dance itself has been mercifully blotted from my memory. I do remember that the only step I was entirely comfortable with was the polka, with its simple step-to-gether, step-together, hop. I employed it for every tune from samba to waltz.

After an eternity, I found myself back on my date's columned porch, and she disappeared into her unimaginable world. Getting into my parents' Olds felt like climbing back into the womb. I don't think I ever said another word to my date, nor she to me. We were like survivors of a disaster who have nothing to link them once the wreckage is cleared away. It would not be for another year, in the seventh grade, that the intermarriage ramifications would present themselves.

The final days of the sixth grade approached, the last year I could catch a reassuring glimpse of my house from across the street. The next year I would attend Chastain Junior High School, a half mile away, and my father would have to acclimate himself to my riding my bike that perilous distance through 1950s suburbia.

It was a hot day in May when our sixth-grade class, all

fifty of us, were called into the auditorium, with its familiar smell of moist mildew attacked but not defeated by Dave's ammonia. It was time for another photograph. We'd all been told the day before to wear a white shirt. We stood on four tiers, fifty white faces, forty-nine white shirts. In this precisely composed photograph, in the back, on the top tier, the smallest boy wore a shirt of darkest green.

My first year in junior high, all the graduates of my dance class were mailed an invitation to attend a rock 'n' roll class. If in the sixth grade I'd seen the dance class as a passport to proximity with the newly fascinating girls in my class, by the seventh grade it was a desperately needed exit visa from my solitude of awkwardness. Suddenly the dance class was all I heard about—at recess on the huge Chastain Junior High playing fields, in the halls as I tried to negotiate changing classes, in the cafeteria that could have held three Boyd cafeterias. I riffled through the mail every day, but the invitation never came. I polled my friends, overheard others talking. I was the only one left out.

I tried to figure out what I had done, what was wrong with me. I was being excluded from the inaugural event of the social whirl and I didn't know how I would ever catch up. Was I that terrible a dancer?

Thirty years later when I told the story to my wife, a southern Christian, she instantly understood what must have happened. My invitation to the sixth-grade dance would have caused a crack in the usual glacial placidity inside my date's coldly columned house. Her parents would have discussed the pairing, however brief and seemingly innocent, of First Baptist Church and Temple Beth Israel. Good manners would have kept them from rescinding their daughter's acceptance, but the next year, with our entering the unmentionable first blush of puberty, it would not have been awkward—merely prudent—to eliminate me as a possible suitor. Given the family's position, a phone call would have been sufficient.

For the twelve weeks that the class was held, I listened as my classmates talked about it. I stood at a distance and watched as they demonstrated the new steps. Sock hops were starting to be held in the junior high gym, and the rock 'n' roll class would have, I thought, given me the compass to navigate the slippery gym floor. But all I knew was the polka.

The farther I ventured into adolescence, the more isolated I felt from my peers. Whereas at Boyd I had merged into the student body, feeling almost as southern as my freckle-faced friends, now I was beginning to have different ideas as I moved from alienation to outright rebellion.

In the ninth grade I subscribed to the *Village Voice*, probably their youngest, possibly their only, subscriber in Mississippi. I don't know how I found out about the then-radical, ultraliberal newspaper—probably through my mother's Sunday *New York Times*, which my father dutifully picked up at a newsstand near the store from a small stack ordered for Jackson's few subscribers desperate for a word from the wide world beyond.

Reading the *Village Voice*, I learned that I was not the only stranger in the world. In the profoundly conservative, segregationist Mississippi of 1962, the *Village Voice* that arrived at my house every week via the U.S. mail would've been viewed by most as a tract personally published by Satan. Yet, though every issue contained subversive ideas and sexual frankness remarkable for those constricted times, my parents raised no objection.

In our house, as in most Jewish homes, books were sacred. They dominated the den and overflowed onto sagging shelves in the guest room. My father seldom read, my mother did constantly, but that wasn't the point. Books, per se, were good, the means both to forget a hostile world and to prevail against it.

My parents placed no restrictions on what I read. Testing them, I announced I wanted to read *Das Kapital* and *Mein Kampf*. My father was concerned, not because I was reading them, but because my name might be connected with them in the library records. My mother dutifully checked them out but I couldn't get beyond the turgid first few pages.

The *Village Voice* showed me a life beyond Mississippi, and I formed the beginning of an escape plan. In the meantime, the place where I found a refuge was the artist's world. Dislocated between cultures, with an artist's imagination, I was always in search of the miraculous.

One night when I was still at Boyd, my mother and I crossed the street to attend a Halloween festival. A few forlorn banners, a sky full of stars, and teachers in costumes were enough to transform the school, in my eyes, into Carnaval in Rio. Throughout Jackson, in the twenty-odd other white elementary schools, the same festival was ongoing. Across town, in another world as unimaginable to me as the Christian world had been only a few years earlier, there must've been something similar going on in the black schools, known then as colored, but so utter was the separation that I could not have named one of their schools any more than I could recite the moons of Jupiter.

As I went from classroom to classroom, I dutifully felt the spaghetti in the bowl (brains) and the grapes (eyeballs), but what I was waiting for was the white elephant sale, which had inflamed my imagination ever since I'd heard about it. It was in a classroom at the end of the hall, marked by a neat sign. How many variations of white elephants could they have? Would any be lifesize? Would some be velvet, others ceramic? Perhaps (it was not altogether out of the realm of possibility) they might actually have a real, live white elephant there for the night and for sale.

When I saw the array of castoff toys, whittled handicrafts, hand-loomed potholders, and other shabby miscellany, the magic of the evening disappeared like a drowned candle. Yet it was my first confirmation that words could conjure a life of dreams, which was where I wished to dwell.

Before I wrote, I drew. As one marked to be an artist, I was not only literally but temperamentally an outcast, and my visions were invariably dark—not placid southern landscapes but oppressed figures crushed by an uncaring universe. I was then fourteen.

One of the few teachers who encouraged my iconoclasm was Mrs. Howell, who taught ninth-grade art. We only took art for a small part of one year (the rest being devoted to more southern subjects, homemaking and shop), but it answered some deep yearning in my divided selves. While other teachers told me to stay between the lines, to do it by the numbers, she hung my paintings on the wall.

My Jewish mother's antennae picked up on the possibility of talent, and she enrolled me in the quintessential southern art class, which proved to be the extinguishment of my painting career. Once a week my mother would drop me off at a cottage in Belhaven, a quaint, quiet neighborhood shaded with old trees. Here I underwent shock therapy for whatever drawing talents I had, administered by a respected local artist, Marie Hull, an imperious painter of ubiquitous magnolias. On the walls throughout her house, and in various stages on every student's canvas, were renditions of the milk-colored, giant-leafed Mississippi state flower. I had no interest in painting it and tried my own ideas. Marie Hull responded with the strongest form of discouragement: she withheld praise, while lavishing it on the young traditionalists around me.

She couldn't help it. To have found some merit in my

anguished squabbles of color would have been as impossible for her as reading the *Village Voice*. After ten weeks, I told my mother I didn't want to go back, and I put away my paints forever.

That September, 1964, I entered Murrah, one of Jackson's three white high schools. The Murrah school district was probably the wealthiest in Mississippi, and Murrah was infamous throughout the state for its rigidly striated caste system. However, wealth alone did not assure popularity at Murrah, nor did junior-ivy-league clothes nor did clean-featured looks, though all of those helped. Football, playing it or cheerleading for it, was what conferred the mantle of grace. Football was sanctified at Murrah, hallowed as a way of life, as it was everywhere in the Deep South.

Growing up, I'd never heard of a Jewish athlete. The idea seemed unnatural and faintly comical, like a bear on a bicycle. I once won a swimming contest, my sole athletic accomplishment, and when my father brought me a towel poolside he was as proud as if I were a championship quarterback. He would have loved for me to join a team, any team, but participating in organized school sports—or following them—was as foreign to me as total-immersion baptism. The fact that everyone else was so obsessed with sports underscored just how much of an outsider I was.

Murrah, like every high school and college in Mississippi, employed numerous coaches. Utterly focused on their teams, they expended their scant remaining resources on their gym classes, which were mandatory for every student. Their lowest priority was the scholastic subjects they'd been dragooned off the playing field to teach, often with little more knowledge of their subjects than their students had. One coach, who taught biology but was besotted with basketball, in describing the human throat inverted the consonants with such certainty when he discussed the "phar*nyx*" and the "lar*nyx*" that I pronounced them incorrectly until adulthood. My driver's education class was taught by a coach whose daily lesson consisted of reading verbatim from a manual from the Mississippi Highway Safety Patrol.

On days of football games, classes were dismissed early so that the coaches, along with uniformed football players and untouchably perfect cheerleaders, could lead massive schoolwide pep rallies. Every Friday afternoon, fifteen hundred students streamed into the Olympic-sized school gym, where blue-and-silver bunting covered the walls and hung from impossibly high rafters, the midnight work of those who had nothing else to contribute. Equine, gun, and cowboy emblems invoked the spirit of the mustang, the team animal. Each coach took his turn at the microphone to stress the epochal significance of the upcoming event, while uniformed players with sombre religiosity urged that victory over Tupelo or McComb or Vicksburg was possible "only if every single one of you is there behind us." Hundreds of high schoolers screamed as one as the Murrah Misses, a marching group of almost-perfect girls, high-stepped in fringed microskirts and white cowboy hats, twirling full-size six-guns.

I didn't want to yell, but I was forced to, by school edict and by the unconflicted full-throated peers surrounding me. It was a mob; worse, it was a group. The pep rallies made me even more uncomfortable than school prayer, where I was only passively violated. Here I had to participate in the pagan festivities.

I tried everything to avoid them—hiding in my classroom, the rest room, the locker room—but the coaches, priests of the faith, allowed no apostasy. Soon I was back in the stands, surrounded by 1499 people who thought, felt, and bellowed as one. My only escape, my only rebellion from the forced conversion, was to scream silently, mouthing the words but allowing no sound to emit.

I thought I might fit in as a writer for the school newspaper, *The Hoofbeat*. I was immediately assigned to the sports section.

My first assignment was to interview a legendary Ole Miss football player, the father of a budding Murrah player. To my fellow southerners, the former athlete was an intrinsically interesting subject, and my article was widely anticipated. As the day of the interview approached, the event assumed outlandish and fearsome proportions in my thoughts. I had only the most elementary knowledge of football; I didn't even know what the positions were. Worse, I had no interest in finding out. In our Jewish household, however, surpassing excellence at every intellectual endeavor was expected (my mother's standard) and it never hurt to know people (my father's). I went to the library to learn about football, but its rudiments eluded me as surely as had the contours of Marie Hull's magnolias.

Finally I compiled a list of very general questions. The Ole Miss legend, a hearty genial man, required no prompting as he recounted the minutiae of his past, and I never got to question two. Listening intently to try to make some sense of it, I scribbled down chaotic notes, knowing I'd have to conjure up some kind of story.

I realized that most southern boys would have cherished these moments with a football great, would have known what he was talking about. But I was an impostor, and the most important thing was hiding that. The next day at school, when asked about the experience, I was elusive, not wanting to give anyone a tour of my tangled psychological terrain. The article I cobbled together, while accurate in a very broad sense, was lacking in nuances that attend comprehension of the material. I knew not to press the masquerade. Next they would have me covering scrimmages, games, God knew what, and I would be unmasked. I resigned from the paper, self-exiled again.

Years later, as a lawyer, I was sent to St. Petersburg, Florida, during spring training to negotiate a contract with baseball great Lenny Dykstra. My law firm was merely an extension of high school, in that the partners were fervent sports followers, for whom a visit to spring training would stand, in their pantheon of memories, alongside (or before) their first sexual experience. On the field, as baseball stars honed their game around me, all I cared about was finishing the job and going home. Back at the firm, when the partners debriefed me for my impressions of the pageantry, and I had none, one lawyer remarked, envious and exasperated, "Pearls before swine." I felt, not for the first time, that my childhood experiences as a stranger were being efficiently recycled for me.

After football season and pep rallies came a more insidious exercise in mass conversion, Character Emphasis Week. For five straight days the entire school was marched into the auditorium to hear a professional motivator lecture us on clean thoughts. He returned every year, the lesson obviously not having taken. The atmosphere was that of a revival tent, and Dr. Chester Something would grow excited, evangelical about clean living, ambition, and, particularly, chastity. He kept his references to Jesus to a minimum, only once every four or five minutes. With the treacly voice of someone who pretends he understands and likes teenagers, he would start every day with a story about some lost teenager (broadly hinting that it had been himself), who had neither lived nor thought cleanly until he had encountered just such an exemplar as was now standing before us.

His presentations invariably ran long and cut deeply into our already-short lunch period. My response varied from the most profound boredom I had yet experienced—far worse than listening to the coach reading the highway patrol statistics—to rage that I was being subjected to, and perhaps influenced, by Dr. Chester. Perhaps his homilies, his warnings, were slipping past my Jewish censor and penetrating my subconscious. I never knew if the other Jews at Murrah felt similarly tormented.

As a group, Jews seemed well-integrated into the student body. When I was a sophomore, Walter Berman, an athlete with his father Max's easy smile, was elected student body president. Unlike Jews in the North or the black students on the other side of town, we were simply too few, perhaps twenty out of a student body of fifteen hundred, to constitute any kind of threat, particularly since we worked so diligently to fit in.

It is a commonplace that everyone remembers where they were when they heard that President Kennedy had been shot. I was at Murrah, about to change class, when the principal came over the P. A. system with the announcement. The response of virtually all my fellow students was immediate jubilant cheering. Though I had admired JFK, was myself stricken by the news, to fit in with my southern classmates cheering the death of a president, I twisted my mouth into an accommodating, agreeing smile.

I was finding it harder and harder to apply Granny's "peace at any price" philosophy. Getting along, going along felt like the shower curtain at the Big House that wrapped itself around you and strangled you. My father became worried about my unpopular and increasingly passionate positions on integration and school prayer. The "in Jesus' name" at the end of the prayers began to feel like a personal assault. As to integration, I enjoyed speaking the blasphemous. I was becoming a South-hating southerner.

I remained a solitary rebel until I met Ralph Salomon through the youth group at Beth Israel. He was tall and spare, with an off-kilter humor, and his family fell on the cultural spectrum farther toward the southern end than mine did. They had come from a small north Mississippi town, and Ralph hunted and fished, which seemed heretical to me. Their Yiddish vocabulary was sparser than my family's, and their southern mangling of the pronunciations even more comical.

These were inconsequential distinctions. When I went to Ralph's (never knocking, just barging in, like at home), I was returning to the large, extended Jewish family I remembered from when I was too young to know anything except where I belonged. Even though these were the teenage years when I was supposedly rejecting everything my parents stood for—the epoch of the "generation gap"—I, like them, found my closest friend from within the tiny population of Jews.

We didn't talk much about our Jewishness—we didn't have to—as we looked for a Tote-Sum that would sell beer to minors, or drove across the Pearl River to the bootleggers (I was barely able to see over the wheel), or circled the parking lot at Shoney's on an always-fruitless safari for girls. We might complain about Rabbi Nussbaum, who terrified Ralph, or about a teacher overheard telling a Jew joke, or some schoolmate's slur and how we had (or more often not) confronted him. Unmentioned was the bond we shared that went back three thousand years.

Ralph and I battled our parents and the school administration over our hair. We were refused entry at a Jackson restaurant, whose owner was determined to single-handedly halt the disintegration of society by refusing to feed anyone with sideburns that extended past a certain point on the ear. Waiters inspected the customers, allowing no appeal and granting no exceptions. Even Eudora Welty, accompanied by a group of longhaired visitors from up north, was turned away, as were national newsmen in town to cover the integration crisis. Long hair was so late coming to the South that by the time Mississippi got around to accepting it, the only people who wore it were those who had persecuted us for it.

Ralph and I were democratic in our insurrections. In the Mississippi Delta town of Cleveland, he and I sneaked out of a youth group meeting in a quixotic search for a beer. The youth group board voted almost unanimously for our suspension, my cousin Roslyn being the only dissenter. I was an unruly element, an outcast even from our own tiny tribe. Something in me made me secede from any group I found myself in.

After Friday night services, which the rabbi required every member of the confirmation class to attend, youth group parties were held at Jewish homes. I was never comfortable at any of these parties, not only because I'd been expelled, but because I didn't want to be seen there. It felt like a ghetto. I didn't want to be Christian—to lose my Jewishness would be like an amputation, a loss of something indefinably central and precious—but at the same time, impossibly, despite my rebellions, I didn't want to be different. That was why, without realizing it, I'd contrived to have myself expelled from the youth group, why I refused to accept them or allow them to accept me.

My high school Christian friends were outsiders like me, seceders from the norm, or we would never have been friends. They always wanted to come over to my house because the simple absence of hell-and-damnation as the bedrock of belief made my house seem a sin-free zone. Once, when I was out of town, a friend racked by a broken love affair sneaked out, came over, and stayed on my phone for hours trying to mend the relationship. It was 2 A.M. before my parents finally turned him out.

In my friends' homes, sex was either never mentioned

or was regarded as a virtual abomination. Because Judaism, unlike southern Protestantism, did not focus on sins of the flesh, for me sex was not a forbidden topic. Sex was natural, I was taught, wonderful, approved by God. I was never told not to have sex, or that there would be repercussions in the afterlife, or even that sex was reserved for marriage. Instead, Judaism, or maybe it was just my father's Jewish motherism, put a novel twist on it. I was told and retold about diseases and pregnancy and how a shotgun marriage could be the end of all my potential. It was more effective a warning than the idea of eternal damnation.

Another reason my friends enjoyed coming over was that they liked my father, who joked comfortably with them when they'd gather to watch *Secret Agent Man* or play poker. Instead of fearing or avoiding him, they sought him out. He was the opposite of their often silent and always authoritarian fathers, and his approachable nature stemmed, at least in part, from the cultural norm in Reform Jewish families for the husband and wife to share much of the power. The fact that my Christian friends were so comfortable in my home made it seem an even safer place.

Although my friends were extremely careful to avoid making anti-Semitic remarks around me, every once in a while something would slip, usually an innocuous comment about how rich Jews were or how cheap. An embarrassed silence would spread over the huge common ground that we didn't share, and I would be faced with the excruciating choice of whether or not to confront them. Since they were my friends I always let it pass. These conflicts I never had to face with Ralph. I began to understand why all my parents' friends were Jewish.

Whenever I was in public—outside my house or another Jewish house—I was aware, however distantly, that I might encounter anti-Semitism. In junior high, two boys nicknamed each other "Rabbi" and "Hebrew" and delighted in using the names in my presence. Because they weren't directly insulting me, I agonized every time over whether to challenge them, always deciding against. In law school at a Baptist college, a student I'd always considered a friend started talking about "Jew lawyers." At a genteel law firm party, I happened onto a circle of partners who were in the middle of telling a Jew joke. Always, the worst of it, after the awkward silence that followed, was having to calibrate each situation, never knowing how or whether to respond or whether the person was a friend or a hidden enemy.

Yet, except for these few experiences, I encountered little anti-Semitism growing up. Though Jews on the east and west coasts tend to consider the South a miasma of Jew-hating, most middle-class Christian acquaintances displayed a carefully wrought tolerance toward us, the same awkward civility I'd witnessed in my mother's ecumenical canasta games.

In our alternate Jewish universe, we had our own stereotypes about southern Christians, based in part on the insularity of the South and in part on my grandparents' experiences in the old country, where often the village Christians were unlettered and violent. My grandparents' view translated itself in my generation to a never-clearly-iterated doctrine: although there were many fine Christians, Jews in general were smarter and were descended from a more ancient civilization.

The physicality of southern Christians—their passion for sports, beauty contests, hunting—appeared to bespeak a lack of reverence for matters of the mind. Even though the ability to perform manual and mechanical tasks might prove useful in day-to-day life, it seemed a matter of pride that we Jews couldn't even change a flat tire.

Because of our tradition, Jews—we believed—didn't go around starting fights or getting drunk, and any Jew who did so was goyish. The Yiddish phrase *shicker ve a goy* ("drunk as a Christian") originated in the old country where Jews rarely drank and Christians usually did; even after the historical basis for the simile had long disappeared, I heard the phrase many times, always applied, without irony, to a sodden Jew.

My family referred to most Christians as "yokels," a word that had many connotations, the most pertinent of which was "provincial." Indeed, many Mississippi Christians were unaware of, and preferred to be unaware of, anything outside the Magnolia State. Other "yokels" were better travelled than we, better educated, more cultured, and wealthier, and yet, because they were not Jewish, they retained for us something of the barbaric, as if at any moment some atavistic attribute of their Pict, Goth, and Vandal forebears might spring forth.

Being in the tiny minority, we never expressed these attitudes in front of Christians. The one exception I remember was an adult gathering of the Cohen cousins I'd grown up with, attended by their Jewish spouses and my southern Christian wife, Kathy. The Cohen men who had grown up in the Big House were in their eighties, all soon to emigrate to join their children scattered throughout the country, and it was the last time they would ever see each other. It was like Sunday at Granny's, except that our own fathers were now the patriarchs.

It was a convivial event with many remembrances. All the Cohens would be leaving Jackson, and for the first time in a century there would be no family presence there except in the cemetery. No one would be left to make sure the Cohen graves were tended to. One of my cousins, secure in the midst of her family and forgetting perhaps that Kathy wasn't Jewish, said, "We'll have to hire some goyim to do it." All laughed, including Kathy.

Kathy wasn't insulted, though she remarked that had such a comment been made about Jews by her family, I would've been outraged at the anti-Semitism. I was never able to persuade her that, because she belonged to the ruling majority, anti-Christianism didn't have the impact or significance of anti-Semitism, though even as I was emphatically making the point it seemed a bit hollow.

"He sure *looks* Jewish."
A former in-law, who was never told I was

Throughout high school I never dated a Jewish girl. Of course, there were very few to choose from. In my Sunday school class of nine, there were three girls, two of whom were cousins. The grade behind me had only one girl, and the year behind that, three or four. Darwinian reality necessitated that I go beyond the tribe. My dating pattern would have seemed of no significance except that, when I later went to a university with a large Jewish student population, I dated a non-Jew for virtually my entire college career, then married twice, each time to a southern Christian.

My parents had been brought up by immigrants, for whom marriage within the faith was viewed as a matter of cultural survival. Although this ethnic Darwinism was taught to me, it reached me diluted and attenuated by a generation. By the time Granny took me aside at a family dinner to which I'd brought my obviously Christian girlfriend and said, without preamble, "You'll only be happy when you marry your own kind," her old compound of guilt and blandishment had long since lost its magic.

While Nell and Sam's grandchildren married Jews, each of Etta and Moise's—Janice, Roslyn, and I—married Christians. Evidence of this curious divide between the two halves of the Cohen family could be traced to Sundays at Granny's, when Moise the *wilde*'s grandchildren were always the unruly, rebellious ones, with the other more conventional side of the family held up as examples of proper obedience and

75

respect. As they grew older, Sam and Nell's grandchildren seemed to have an unconflicted Jewish identity, while mine remained contested ground.

As a senior I attended a football game where I saw my cousin Gary, an insecure sophomore, dressed in coat and tie, on what he later described as his sole high school date. My father and Lazar were like brothers, and the relationship had continued another generation. Gary and I shared Sundays at Granny's, the store in which our fathers were partners, outrage at the imbecilities of Mississippi politics, and an all-consuming mail-order stamp business. (Cohen Stamp Distributors was the ambitious name for our miniscule but grandiosely conceived mail-order philatelic operation, which we had operated for years from a table in the second-floor alterations area of the store. We advertised in all the national stamp publications, and none of our customers guessed they were doing business with two children.)

Though smaller than Gary, I was older and had allowed my training in karate to create a reputation far in excess of my actual martial ability. So I was sometimes Gary's protector, a fact that made what I did that night all the more inexplicable. As Gary sat on the very back row with his Christian date, I began loudly calling him a Jew. Acting under color of intoxication, but nowhere near as drunk as I pretended to be, I repeated it again and again, as he sat, mortified, begging me to be quiet.

"Hey, everybody, there's a Jew over here." Fellow students around us stared. Leaning close to his date, I asked her conspiratorially, "Do you know Gary is a Jew?" Gary sat hunched over, enduring it like all our ancestors had done, until I, his brother and protector, finally subsided and wandered away, convinced I had been hilarious.

Gary ceased speaking to me, and I rationalized that he had overreacted. It was awkward working together every Saturday at the store, meeting every Sunday at Granny's, even more painful using the few words necessary to split up the stamp stock of Cohen Stamp Distributors. For an entire year Gary didn't speak to me, until one day Lolita, as always the catalyst, took me aside.

"You two have been too close for too many years," she said. "All he wants is an apology."

I'd been looking for a way to bridge the break between us. I gestured for him to follow me outside. Warily he joined me in front of the store. Within moments he had accepted my apology, and at lunch we had a year's worth of family anecdotes and stamp lore to share. Cohen Stamp Distributors was reborn, to the delight of our six customers nationwide.

What I didn't express in my apology, what I still couldn't understand, was why I had done it. Was I parodying prejudice, co-opting it, like blacks calling each other "nigger"? Or was I using Gary as an external target for my internal rage at myself for being different, shouting to Gary what I wouldn't think to myself, that I didn't want to be Jewish? Whatever the cause, my tangled identity cost me a brother for a year.

In the eleventh grade, I got into a fistfight at school, the quick escalation of a hallway scuffle. The incident brought me squarely up against the southern sacrament of fighting and my own conflicted feelings about it.

The southerners I grew up with, heirs to the code duello, had a prickly sense of honor and a tradition of physically defending it. This side of southern culture flourished in the drive-in beer bars way out North State Street, a row of ramshackle taverns like the Shamrock and the Cherokee and the Red Top, where working-class adults drank inside, while outside underage customers like me waited in our cars to be served by even younger black boys. These black children were viewed as beneath the law and thus could act as middlemen.

Once beer had softened the membrane of the drinkers' pride, making it permeable to any imagined slight, more beer hardened the language, so that the insults often weren't imagined. A night at the Shamrock potentially held both the excitement of witnessing a fight and the fear of being in one, of rolling around in the gravel until the manager broke it up with a curse and all our cars went flying to the next spot down the road.

The ready southern recourse to violence contrasted utterly with the traditional Jewish attitude, which seemed to have been imported without alteration from eastern Europe, where our ancestors had been helpless victims of pogroms. What got translated through the generations and over the ocean was a cultural view that physical fighting was crude, dangerous, and, worst of all, goyish.

The day of my fight at school, I felt someone step on my heel, hard, from behind. I looked up sharply as a large gangly senior passed me. The scuff had apparently been inadvertent, but it was also without apology. The kid was a good bit bigger than I, and I didn't want to fight him. I'd almost never been in a fight (excepting the time in Sunday school when I hit a classmate who called me a communist), but, as a southerner, I couldn't let the dishonor stand. I split the difference between my two halves and intentionally stepped on his heel, hoping it would be taken as accidental.

It wasn't. Now his honor had been sullied, and within moments we were outside, fists up, while an eager crowd quickly gathered. Fighting in the Jackson public school system in those days had its own primitive Marquis of Queensbury rules. The basic rule was "fight fair." That meant no sticks or broken bottles, no kicking, no hitting when your opponent was down, and stopping when one said, "I give." Compared to fights I'd heard about in the urban jungles of northern schools, ours were quaintly civilized. We exchanged a few punches—he landed a wild hook near my eye, I jabbed his nose, bringing a gush of blood. The fight ended inconclusively, fizzling out as the class bell rang and the crowd dispersed, giving both combatants an honorable exit.

As my bruise darkened, I worried about how my parents would react. I reassured myself by remembering that Moise had thrown rocks, that my father had always said to stand up for yourself, and that his nickname was "Tiger," earned at Tulane when he decked a man who hit one of his fraternity members brought up on the pogrom model of Jewish self-defense. I didn't know how all that squared with the other, the Jewish, tradition.

My father, the southerner, only wanted to know one thing: had I given as much as I'd gotten? Victory wasn't important. All that Tiger required was that I hadn't let anyone push me around. My mother, from her more Jewish end of the spectrum, wanted to know the ethical considerations, including who began the fight, the answer to which was murky. Even so, she'd heard her own tales from Poland, and her father had nearly died in Shreveport when the robber cracked his skull with the Seven-Up bottle; she let my goyish behavior pass.

I never went hunting, in fact had never fired a gun, which put me at a vast distance from most of my male classmates at Murrah, for whom hunting was intrinsic to their upbringing. In the fall they often faced a difficult choice, when the year's first college football game clashed with another southern sacrament, the opening day of dove season. Two months later, around Thanksgiving, deer season was a time of ritual bonding between father and son.

I was only vaguely aware of these central events in my classmates' lives. I'd heard of the bar mitzvah-like rite of passage of a boy's first kill, listened to stories of bathless days in deer camp unrestrained by civilization.

In our house, we treasured civilization. It was what we relied upon in the Christians around us for their forebearance. Hunting seemed not merely physical but primitive. My father had a pistol from his World War II days in China and India, kept to repel burglars, but its exact location was not known to anyone.

We did know of Jews who hunted. Ralph did, and by unspoken agreement we never talked about it. Some Jewish doctors were ardent hunters, prompting my mother's irritated wonderment. "They work all day to save lives," she observed, "so they can spend their time off killing."

She identified with the prey, and so did I, as I had learned many years earlier when I was nine and my father took me fishing at a small muddy lake near Jackson. He was no sportsman, but I'm sure his intent was that we should have a normal southern experience like the other children with their fathers at the lake. He undertook the baiting, an act of courage on his part because of his fear of being impaled by the hook and having to get a tetanus shot.

We settled into fishing, an average southern father and son by all appearances, relaxing on the clay mud shore. Conceivably, we could've been talking of our best hunting dog and how he had treed a panther or raccoon (though I knew that raccoons, and also squirrels, were carriers of rabies). Or we could've been looking forward to the mess of fish my mother was going to skin, clean, and deep-fry once she got through with her canasta game. All around the lake were fathers and sons having some kind of uncomplicated experience, but as for me, I was thinking, what in God's name am I doing here, holding this pole with a roach pinned to the end of a hook? And, worse: what if I catch a fish?

One of the nearby fishermen remarked that they weren't

biting today, and I began to relax. Yet the tranquility of fishing, of sitting wordless for a long time in the same place holding a pole with a roach at the end, genetically eluded me. My mind, even at nine, was whirling around, wondering why I wasn't enjoying it.

After a couple of hours, as the sun began to set, my father concluded that we'd had a good healthy experience, and we prepared to leave. That was when I felt a tug on the end of my pole.

"Pull him in, pull in him!" my father encouraged, excited, his southern self taking over. I dragged a tiny fish from the life-giving muddy broth of the lake. While the fish gasped, my father determined that it was too small to keep. I was joyous. The fish would live. At this point my memory becomes jumbled. There was some impediment, some indecision. Perhaps my father didn't know how to get the hook out.

A man with a stubble of beard approached. "I'll take it," he said. Despite my father's southern side, he was far out of his world here, and I didn't have time or courage to protest before I heard him accede. Without ceremony the man threw my fish into his bucket, where it thrashed loudly and hopelessly for a long time.

Years later I understood my father's capitulation when a similar experience allowed me to redress the crime against my poor fish. To do so, I had to stand up to over two hundred years of southern precedent—and a century of Jewish assimilation—and reveal myself as an utter misfit.

It was early morning. I'd returned from the kitchen to the bedroom to dress for work when something gigantic flapped past my face, shrieking. I retreated, closing the door behind me, and listened as it careened through the room, knocking over lamps, beating against the windows, banging into every wall. I risked a look. A very large mallard had somehow plunged down the chimney into my bedroom.

As a nonhunter, my only previous experience with ducks had been with the very tame, disciplined ones that paraded from the elevator to the fountain in the lobby of the Peabody Hotel in Memphis. This duck, however, was twice the size of the Peabody variety, with a wingspread that seemed pterodactylene in the small room. It had crapped all over my bed and was now tearing at the window, beating its green-and-black wings like Leda's swan about to consummate itself with my Levolar blinds.

A true southerner would've known what to do, how to subdue it physically, with a net or coat or bare hands. As for me, I reclosed the door and went to the phone book, hoping there was some governmental agency that might assist me with this natural disaster. Remarkably, there was just such a listing—Small Animal Control.

Within twenty minutes S.A.C. arrived, consisting of a shriveled, berry-tan white woman supervising a rotund black man. The man, without fear, entered my bedroom. He returned momentarily.

"Fat one."

He reentered with a net, there was increased fluttering, another lamp fell, and he emerged with the duck struggling in the net.

"What are you going to do with it?" I ventured.

"He'd make good eating," the assistant said, more to his supervisor than to me.

"I don't know," the berry-tan woman responded, the first words she'd uttered.

They argued the matter. Although the official policy, as I gathered from their colloquy, was to free captured wildlife, the unspoken cultural norm was the opposite. The supervisor seemed to be swayed by the man's reasoning while I watched, late for work, a helpless bystander to this life-and-death situation. I didn't want to appear un-macho, un-southern. Remembering that now-mythical day on the lake with my father and the small fish, I made myself speak.

"I thought you were supposed to let them go."

They looked at me, irritated at my intervention. I was wearing a tie. Who knew how big a pain in the ass I might be? Finally the woman ungraciously said they'd follow procedure. They put the duck into their official Small Animal Control truck and drove off. I had to be sure, so I stayed right behind them, all the way to Mayes Lake, until the moment they set my duck free. My childhood fish was not forgotten, but at least in my Jewish ledgerbook he had been balanced.

This tenderness—I don't know what other word to use—for helpless creatures I learned from my mother. When I was a child, she would watch for hours through the den window as her private wild zoo gathered to eat the food she set out. She was furious at the blue jays for chasing off the smaller birds. We'd sit together and watch the squirrels move in jump-cuts along the pine branches. She was elated when a small brown rabbit joined her afternoon assemblage.

We guessed at how it survived, surrounded by a hostile world. I imagined its life and knew it hid in some thicket of cut branches, or a hole too small for dogs, and that it risked everything to emerge from hiding. It had come for a week, becoming more and more domesticated, letting my mother get near it, staying longer each time. One day when I came home from school, my mother was in her familiar place on the sofa, looking out the den window, but something was different.

"He didn't come today," she said with her usual fatalism. I felt an inordinate sadness.

"He'll be back," I said. But as usual she was right.

The Temple

For you are a chosen people, exalted among all others.
From the Jewish book of prayer

"If you don't eat the hard-boiled egg, you have to leave the Passover seder."
Rabbi Perry E. Nussbaum, speaking to me when I was nine

When my grandparents came to the United States, they brought with them the same Judaism they'd been taught in Europe. It was close in practice and stringency to what is practiced today by Orthodox Jews who observe kosher dietary laws, wear yarmulkes, and recite copious amounts of Hebrew in their services.

The Judaism my grandparents encountered in the South was Reform Judaism, by far the most liberal, assimilated form of the faith. They adapted quickly to the Americanized Judaism, and in fact were much more comfortable with this relaxed level of observance. Even this degree of devotion was often too constricting for Tottie, who would take me by the hand and lead me outside to the front steps, where he smoked a cigarette and I breathed free air. Those fugitive moments with my grandfather were magical, and my earliest memories of religion are of escape.

Around that time, I discovered a small mysterious box hidden in a drawer. Wrapped in tissue paper was the strangest thing I'd ever seen—a small leather square, with black straps trailing it like multiple tails. It looked like a museum specimen of some extinct creature, and in a way it was. Intrigued with its oddity, and also a little frightened because it was so alien, I brought it to my mother. It was Tottie's tefillin, she said, used by Orthodox Jews in prayer. The box contained scripture and was strapped to the head, while other straps were wrapped around the forearms. More than that my mother didn't know, except that the box had never been opened by Tottie since he came to America. I put the tefillin back in the drawer, unaccountably fascinated with it, yet also very glad that my grandfather didn't engage in such strange practices.

Our pasteurized, homogenized Judaism, with as much exoticism as possible pared away, was thoroughly attuned to the unvoiced desires of southern Jews to fit in. Whereas northern synagogues were distinctively Jewish, our temples were designed to look like churches. On Saturday, the Jewish Sabbath, as Orthodox Jews in the North were walking to all-day services, we were playing just like our Christian counterparts; our Sabbath, migrating southward, had switched itself to Sunday. And while the Orthodox prayerbooks presented thick forests of Hebrew, our prayerbooks planted bits of Hebrew like ornamental trees of authenticity. The bedrock prayers of the faith, such as the Sh'ma ("Hear O Israel, the Lord our God, the Lord is one") we did say in southern-accented Hebrew, but it was spelled out for us phonetically so that even the most assimilated of us could participate.

Sometimes the rabbi would hack his way through the sections of untranslated Hebrew, but when it came time for the responsive reading by the congregation, virtual silence would fall over the sanctuary, broken only by the few Orthodox Jews present. Because there was no Orthodox temple in Jackson, they were reduced to worshipping with us and subsisting on our attenuated religious fare.

The Orthodox Jews seemed as alien to me as Christians. The stories about them that filtered down to me were frightening; I heard about one father who sat shiva, performing the prayer for the dead, when his son married a Christian, and I felt fortunate that my parents did not adhere to such a harsh unyielding faith. When I saw the man in temple, I was afraid of him.

My Christian schoolmates went to Sunday school, as did we, but what we were taught once we were safely inside Temple Beth Israel would have been regarded by them as heretical, sacrilegious, blasphemous.

From age five, when we started Sunday school, until age fifteen, when we were confirmed, we basically ignored what was the central occurrence for the rest of western civilization, the birth of Jesus. Though we conceded that a historical figure such as Jesus probably had existed, he took up little class time during my ten years of Sunday school. Our teachers made no attempt to refute the view that he was the Son of God. It was simply assumed that we all knew this claim was untrue. Our biblical ancestors hadn't seen any reason to change what they had believed for a thousand years when a few zealots started trumpeting a new dispensation, and two thousand years of Christian ascendancy hadn't supplied any more compelling arguments.

Nor was the New Testament discussed in Sunday school. Our list of books of the Bible stopped dead at Malachi. Matthew, Mark, and all the rest were like the blank spaces of terra incognita on old maps: places of myth and fantasy, never to be visited. The New Testament was not even taught as history, and we Jews have always been hungry for history. We were told that these unsanctioned biblical addenda existed—but never what was in them. Perhaps our teachers feared that if we knew we might go sailing off the end of the world.

I had no idea what was going on in the Baptist and Methodist churches that seemed to be on every block in Jackson. When my parents drove me to Sunday school, we were caught in a polite version of rush hour traffic. In the cars ahead of me, behind me, in the next lane, were scrubbed little Christian boys in clip-on ties, pigtailed girls in ribbons and frills, parents literally in their Sunday best. I watched them park in giant parking lots, stream into church after church as we drove by, the children much better behaved than we, the parents somehow more reverent. I was boggled by the sheer *numbers* of them. At every church we passed, there was a sign, changed weekly, featuring a quotation about Jesus. I asked my parents what was going on in there, but they knew as little as I.

When we arrived at Beth Israel's parking lot—unimpressively gravelled and, though small, rarely full—I saw not so much a stream of worshippers as a reluctant spritz. There would be parents cajoling and threatening their children to go in, children hovering outside the door with their friends until the last possible moment, and many latecomers, unchastened, always the same ones.

Our Sunday school class was larger than most; we had sometimes eight or nine in our grade while others had only three or four. The emphasis in our religious school was more on the "school" aspect than the "religious," the opposite of Christian Sunday schools. We were not there for worship but for the imparting of knowledge. Every Sunday from 10:00 until 12:15 we learned about history, ethics, anti-Semitism. We had tests, essays, and grades. While Christian classes, I learned years later, might end with all praying or else singing "Jesus Loves Me," our class would conclude with the homework assignment, which generally was never done (we were, after all, southern Jews).

Throughout my Sunday school career I was never certain about the Jewish position on God. The explicit teaching, of course, was that there was a God and that we had been the first to perceive him. Yet there seemed to be a certain ambivalence in the Sunday school lessons about the fundamental question of God's existence. Perhaps when all the exoticism had been pared from our service, a bit of God had gone with it.

Biblical events taught to my Christian classmates as holy and actual were cast for us as historical or allegorical. In my early years of Sunday school the accounts of the burning bush and the crossing of the Red Sea were simply spread before us as children's stories. Later, when our teachers judged we had attained some measure of the supreme Jewish virtue, reason, we learned that it was possible that such things could, theoretically, be made to happen by a God who was all-powerful. However, our teachers provided more logical explanations. For example, the Red Sea referred to in Exodus was probably a much smaller stream whose waters were known to part for perfectly good scientific reasons. There simply was no room for the miraculous; we had to have our wits about us to survive.

As to what we were taught about Jesus, I'm not sure whether my mother inoculated me before I began Sunday school or whether she gave me prophylactic booster shots to supplement what I was taught. As my mother explained it, Jesus was a great prophet, though, she would add, not the greatest prophet. But that was all he was. Everyone else had gotten carried away, and we Jews were the only ones who had remained levelheaded. That's what I had learned, specifically from my mother and generally from everyone else in the family, and it was reinforced in snatches of canasta conversation and Sunday school lessons. I was corrected if, by accident, adopting the common parlance, I referred to him as "Jesus Christ." "Christ" meant "savior," I was told, and we were still waiting for him, although I don't think my supremely rational-minded mother expected him to arrive any time before Godot.

I didn't know quite what to do with the fact that Jesus had been Jewish. It was a source of pride that someone so esteemed by my Boyd classmates and half the entire world was Jewish. As Jesus' life progressed, however, he somehow ceased to be a practicing Jew and became a Christian. At least that was my understanding. When the pantheon of Notable Jews throughout History—Moses, Spinoza, Einstein—was heralded in Sunday school class, Jesus was not included. It was as if we were sitting shiva for him.

I gained a bare smattering of knowledge about my fellow southerners' faith from the half-year our Sunday school devoted in the eighth grade to comparative religion. All the other faiths were treated respectfully. It was basic to Judaism that there was no one path to the truth. At least that was the overt message. Somehow it was also conveyed that there was one path—ours—that was more direct and less intellectually compromised with folkloric superstitions such as virgin births and resurrections.

I supplemented my Sunday school material with a giant *Life* book, *The World's Great Religions*. I was proud to see that Judaism was one of the "big six," even if not numerically. The big glossy photos of Catholic masses and Protestant baptisms were as exotic to me as depictions of Confucian ancestor worship or Moslems swirling around the Kaaba in Mecca.

Beth Israel was not a reverent congregation. At the weekly Friday night services (all that remained of the traditional sundown-Friday-to-sundown-Saturday observance), the congregants' greetings, which started before the service, developed into over-the-pew gossiping once it began. At any one time during the service, eight or nine whispered conversations might be ongoing, with negligible peer pressure to be quiet. It was as if, unmoored from and unsupervised by the centers of Judaism in the North, all the adults became children eager to commune with their extended kin after a week of immersion in the Christian world.

Stepping inside the temple was like being transported to

another dimension, one that was not defined by height or width or depth but by an equally pervasive factor, Jewishness. The transition was immediate. One moment I was outside, subject to all the perceived diminishments of the Christian world. The next moment, it all fell away and I felt like I was back at home on Brook Drive, in a much-expanded but equally all-Jewish universe. Once again, I knew that no one around me would make an anti-Semitic comment. The hermetically sealed worlds of Brook Drive, the canasta games, the temple, and vacations to Miami Beach and the Catskills were carefully constructed temporary fortresses where we might never have to meet a Christian.

As a child, I found it enormously comforting to sit with my parents, surrounded by Etta and Moise and the rest of the Cohens, in a room that held nothing but Jews as far as the eye could see. It was possible to pretend that the world was this way; knowing that it wasn't made the solidarity even greater. It was reassuring to see the canasta ladies, accompanied by their poker-playing husbands. After the service, everyone turned to those all around and murmured "Good Shabbas" ("Good Sabbath") and shook hands or kissed. As we made our way up the aisle to say "Good Shabbas" to the rabbi, some of the canasta ladies would enfold me with warm hugs.

Paradoxically, attendance at temple was often sparse. My parents went perhaps one Friday a month, sometimes less. The congregation was too small to exert the social pressure that nudged our Christian neighbors to their houses of worship on Sundays and on Wednesday prayer nights. Our temple simply didn't possess the gravitational pull to draw my parents out of their private Jewish island on Brook Drive. For us, Sundays at Granny's constituted religious service enough.

Though it seemed interminable to such a restive congregation, the Friday night service actually was fairly brief, perhaps an hour, depending on the rabbi and how seriously he took his duties to sermonize. It began with the kiddush, the lighting of the Sabbath candles, done by congregants summoned to the pulpit to struggle through the phoneticized Hebrew blessing with their southern accents, sometimes having to be helped over a syllable or two by the rabbi. There was a good bit of standing up and sitting down and long sections of narrative. For the responsive reading, the congregation was entrusted only with the English, while the Hebrew Union College-trained rabbi navigated through the Hebrew. I kept one finger in the back of the prayer book, watching the pages decrease at the rate it takes a watched pot to boil.

In shedding all the old-fashioned and embarrassing Hebraic mystery, the service had also lost some of its emotional heart. Yet some majesty remained in our pared-down, anglicized, and sparsely attended Friday night services. Despite myself, I would often be captured by the solemn poetry of the prayers, particularly the ones that seemed to speak of a special relationship with God and offered an explanation of why we had to be different.

The austerity of the temple's architecture was mirrored in the almost existential courage of the prayers. A religion that frankly states it does not know whether there is an afterlife brought forth my grudging admiration at the same time I resented the lack of any comfort. It was all intertwined with my mother somehow. When I asked her before she died whether she believed there was a heaven, she voiced the view I'd heard every Friday night in my youth: "You live on in the hearts of those who remember you." And that was it. What a responsibility for those who remained, and what breathtaking strength it required of the ones about to depart.

At every Friday night service, the rabbi read the names of those whose *yahrzeit*, anniversary of death, had fallen that week. This commemoration was for me the most poignant moment of the service. When I was young, I recognized none of the names. Then, as I grew up, more and more frequently I did, and for the moment their names were read I would indeed remember them, see them—Lolita's round-faced mother, Rose, the frail sharp-eyed Mr. Martin, who had reminded me of Tottie, Victor Glick, who had no family and gave me his stamp collection—and so under Jewish tradition they would, at least for that brief time, live on. When the time came for Tottie's *yahrzeit* and for Rae's, my mother would always go to services, as did my father when Moise's and Etta's names were read. Because our family was normally so unobservant, their unfailing attendance emphasized for me what a sacred duty it was, this act of remembrance, the gift of life.

Midway through the service would come a private meditation. The prayer book gave an example but then stated, "or such other prayer as the heart may prompt." Sitting between my parents on the unadorned wooden pew, I looked to them for guidance as to what I should do in this uncharted section of the service.

My father's eyes as often as not weren't closed. When I thumbed to the back of the prayer book to see how much farther, he had already pioneered that journey and had his fourth finger firmly implanted there as a goal. If his eyes were closed, I could guess what he might be praying for—good business at the store, safety for my mother and me. But I could never fathom what my mother, closed within herself as always, might be praying for, some private thing that I would never know.

It is the memory of my mother that I most associate with Friday night services. When I was a child, my favorite place to be during the service was beside her when she sang in the choir. We'd walk up a narrow dusty staircase; musty, ancient-seeming, as if it had been there since biblical times, it was made of the same dark unadorned wood as the rest of the temple. I imagined such woods had constituted the interiors of the First and Second Temples in Jerusalem.

The choir sat in a small alcove above the pulpit. There my mother and two other volunteers from the congregation were led by a professional, a redoubtable-looking woman named Magnolia Coulet. No matter how many times I heard Magnolia sing, it was always a shock to behold her dextrous familiarity with the Hebrew songs, a fluency that far surpassed what most of the Jews sitting below could manage. She was a sweet-natured woman, and I felt somehow honored that she would have taken the time to master the intricacies of our secret language. Our club was so small that it needed as many members as it could recruit. My mother's singing voice was a clear, unwavering soprano, much sweeter than her speaking voice, or so it seemed to me. It was as if when she was safe in that little choir room, carried along with ancient songs familiar from her own childhood, she didn't need the edge in her voice that was her only protection against a hurtful world.

I, too, felt protected in that cozy alcove. I could peek over the top of the wall and look down at the top of the rabbi's bald head, then out into the congregation at my father. No one could see me. It was a secret kingdom, and with it came the sanctioned waiver of any requirement to follow the service. Whenever the choir sang, I sat, entranced by the metamorphosis in my mother's voice. Between songs, when the rabbi droned on below, I would listen to the choir's whispered conversations or drop off to sleep. It was deliciously illicit, like skipping school with no chance of penalty.

Almost all the Jews I encountered at Beth Israel, at Friday night services or as Sunday school teachers, were as southern as my parents. Many, like my father, were lifelong Beth

Israel members. Others had gravitated to Jackson, the largest city in the state, from small towns in the Mississippi Delta, hastening the ultimate closure of once-vibrant congregations there. Still others, through marriage or work, had moved from larger southern cities such as Memphis, New Orleans, and Atlanta, though culturally I couldn't differentiate them from homegrown congregants. Dr. Max Berman, from Georgia, with his gigantic glasses of iced tea, had the same easygoing, southern graces as the three genteel Lehman girls, Phyllis, Bea, and Celeste, who were born only a buggy ride from my father on Fortification Street.

Others had migrated from the North. When I first encountered them at temple, I was confounded. Their names were Jewish, they were undoubtedly Jews, yet they were almost as foreign as the Christian canasta ladies. Not that they were reserved. Rather, they were louder than the Cohens, more impatient, their speech peppered with more Yiddishisms. Their edges had not been softened, their directness had not been diverted, their ethnicity had not been diluted by a sojourn in the land of their cultural opposites.

They also seemed smarter. Their no-nonsense clipped consonants, their nasal *a*'s, the speed at which they did and said everything though there was no pressing need, spoke to me of some greater efficiency, a linkage with the intellectual engines of the North while we sat stupefied in a past not even our own.

Some of the northern Jews in the temple came to Jackson, no doubt reluctantly, as the result of a job transfer. Most, however, had marriage to blame.

Of the five Cohen children in the Big House, three married southern Jews. My mother was from Shreveport; Lazar's wife, Lolita, had been born in Canton just a few miles up Highway 51 from Jackson; and Marvin had married a girl with an exotic New Orleans accent. The other two Cohens had married Yankees. Buddy's wife, Ann, was from Chicago, and Aunt Pearle's husband, Uncle Melvin, was a lawyer from Boston ("A professional man!" Granny had exulted).

All of them were absorbed into the Cohen family, as if swallowed whole by an embracing anaconda. The shape of the family got stretched, not only by the five new personalities but by the new northern culture.

Uncle Melvin had gone to an Ivy League school and seemed somehow to know more about things, Jewish and non-Jewish, than our homegrown Cohens. Yet the South suited him, and he soon found himself naturally in rhythm with its undemanding pace. He gave up his law practice and settled comfortably into working in the store alongside Moise, Sam, Lazar, and my father. Whatever his religious training had been up north, he soon slid into our lax practice. After a few years, he seemed as southern as my father.

Not so my cousin Ann, who married Buddy. She'd been brought up to keep the kosher dietary rules: separate plates for meat and dairy, abstention from pork and shellfish, specially trained butchers who slaughtered and blessed the beef in a very particular way. In the large Jewish centers up north, there was no shortage of such butchers nor of peer pressure to make the whole process seem normal.

In the South, my grandparents, by necessity but also by liberating choice, embraced all things American. Kosher had fallen away, geographically, somewhere between the mid-Atlantic and the Mason-Dixon line. In Jackson, keeping kosher seemed as bizarre and antiquated as sacrificing a goat on a mountaintop.

For my cousin Ann to keep kosher, as with any of the northern Jews who found themselves in the southern wilderness, compromises had to be made. Dogma was diluted. First went the blessed beef, then the separate plates. Shrimp, so fresh from the gulf, might be grudgingly allowed onto some tables. All that was left was pork, and there the cultural erosion stopped. The long arm of religious law reached all the way from eastern Europe and snatched from Cousin Buddy's plate his juicy spicy sausage patties, his fried pork chops and, mercilessly, even his bacon.

I never knew how confining kosher could be until the summer we went to the Catskill Mountains in upstate New York, the epicenter of Jewish vacationing in those days. At resorts such as Grossinger's and the Concord, a totally Jewish experience was assured, from fellow guests to entertainment to diet. Several kosher suppers taught me that the approved cuts of beef were less succulent than the strip sirloins and filets on which I'd been raised. I yearned for ice cream, cheese, even milk, which at home my mother had to force down me.

Driven by the same hungers as I, my father investigated and learned that far out on the Concord golf course was a clubhouse. It, like Dixieland, was so far away from the hub that dietary restrictions were lax or even nonexistent. Like Moses' Israelites in reverse, we walked along the fairways, the imposing-looking Concord receding in the distance, until we saw a small, unprepossessing building filled with slightly guilty-looking though unrepentant guests, renegades escaping the iron kosher fist. That night at dinner, as I picked at a tasteless kosher chicken, I was sustained by the knowledge that the next day my father and I would again visit the land of milk and honey and cheeseburgers.

In Jackson, over the years, the resolve of most of the northern Jewish spouses was weakened by distance and time and surrounding custom. Two million Mississippians to one were not impossible odds, for Jews had regularly faced much greater challenges, but when the fellow three hundred bacon-eating Jackson Jews were added to the scale, the final barrier came down. As the Hormel sugar-cured bacon sizzled and spat in frying pan after frying pan, some invisible cultural metamorphosis was taking place.

* * *

No such metamorphosis had softened the stringent practices of my mother's northern relatives, as I learned during an unforgettable visit to Jackson from my great-uncle Sig.

Unlike my grandmother Rae, Uncle Sig had fiercely adapted to the new land. A warmhearted but choleric man used to getting his way, he had forged a considerable scrap business empire in Kansas City. In fact, all of Rae's four brothers became wealthy. Only Rae, the one who looked back, the daughter left to care for the parents, died young and poor.

Kansas City was well outside the ambit of southernized Reform Judaism, and the faith Uncle Sig practiced had been imported without diminution from his shtetl in Poland. Candles were lit every Friday night. The Sabbath was honored, and it was on Saturday. On Rosh Hashanah and Yom Kippur, he spent the whole day in temple, as prescribed. Uncle Sig was visiting us for Passover, the celebration of the deliverance of the Jews from slavery in Egypt, traditionally observed in the home with a dinner and service, the seder. Passover falls around Easter, a time of year in the Deep South when the weather is treacherously unpredictable.

Our mammoth central air-conditioning system occupied an entire small room, like one of the gigantic 1950s protocomputers. It was the most modern unit available, its dull hum as essential as an iron lung. None of my friends at Boyd had central air. The most they had was a single feeble window unit, a fact that I construed as another significant distinction between Christians and Jews.

We had no window units. As modern Jews, we placed our faith in the new technology, and the massive contraption was our sole protection against the relentless summer that covered Mississippi like a damp blanket for almost half the year, from late April when the azaleas faded until early October when the state fair arrived and with it the first breath of cool weather.

Our unit's technology was primitive, its nature temperamental, and several times each summer I awakened knowing something was very wrong. I heard no hum. I felt the heat around me, clutching me. Soon I saw the lights go on in the hall and listened as my father opened the door to the air-conditioning room.

Often the repairman couldn't get there for days. All the windows were thrown open to catch the hot listless breeze. When the repairman finally came, frequently a part had to be ordered "from Memphis," and we waited for it like pioneers at the end of the Pony Express route.

Whenever the seasons changed, the unit had to be switched from "heat" to "cool" or back by a technician. It was apparently a fairly intricate procedure, far beyond the mechanical skills of our Jewish household. Once the unit was set on "heat" for the winter, its cooling function was inoperable, hibernating until spring when the technician resuscitated it.

Every year we had to guess and gamble on when to make the switch. The year my uncle Sig arrived to conduct the seder, we had guessed wrong. The unit was still set on "heat," and the temperature at noon when he began the service was already well into the nineties. By the time that endless, muggy day was over, we felt as though we'd weathered forty years in the desert.

Our Haggadah, the prayer book for the Passover celebration, was over fifty pages thick with prayers, songs, and narrative readings that preceded a festive meal. It continued after the meal for another sixty-eight pages.

The Haggadah had never daunted our family of southernized Jews. My mother had without remorse gone through each prayer book and paper-clipped the sections she subjectively thought caught the essence of the service.

Neatly typed and inserted in each Haggadah was her abridgement:

1. Light Candle lights, p. 3
2. Say Kiddush, p. 4
3. P. 16
4. P. 18, Section 4
5. P. 48
6. P. 50

The service clocked out at around twelve minutes.

We held the seder every year with Aunt Pearle and Uncle Melvin and their daughters, Janice and Roslyn, then ages twelve and ten. Often yelling and screaming at some perceived outrage, my cousins were *wildes*, like our grandfather, Moise, and when I was under their evil influence, the term was applied to us by the entire family, not altogether lovingly.

That Passover, we all gathered in the small dining room that was normally the poker parlor, the windows wide open on a day that was as still as it was hot. I saw the sunlight refracting through the palpable humidity. Nine of us sat close together around the dining room table as Uncle Sig picked up his Haggadah.

The first warning sign was his yarmulke; the next was that he began at the top of page one and continued sequentially, unlike my mother, whose abridged service skipped ten, twenty, or more pages at a whack before arriving at the instruction "Serve the Passover meal."

On Uncle Sig went, through every cup of sweet Mogen David wine, every responsive reading. Beads of sweat gathered on his brow as he passionately read not only the Hebrew, which for us just constituted page filler, but also the English versions of every prayer. Janice and Roslyn were pressed into reading the lengthy Four Questions about Passover that every child should ask each year but that we had

Top left: Moise, 1909 / Top right: Etta, 1909 /
Bottom left: Rae, in Poland, c. 1912 / Bottom right: Ben, in Poland, c. 1912

Top left: Edward's great-grandfather, who emigrated from Poland to America, then turned right around and went back / Top right: Lazar, Buddy, and Leonard, 1917 / Bottom (top to bottom): Lazar, Buddy, Marvin, Pearle, and Leonard, at the Big House, 1922

Top: Marcia, sister-in-law, and Pauline, Jones Beach, New York, 1944 / Bottom left: Pauline, in the WAVES, New York, 1944 / Bottom right: Leonard, in the Air Force, China-Burma-India Theatre, 1944

Top left: Edward as *shaygitz*, 1952 / Top right: the *Wildes*, Janice, Edward, and Roslyn, at Granny's, 1952 / Right center: Edward with Gladys, Jackson, 1949 / Bottom: Edward with his parents at Roosevelt Hotel, New Orleans, 1958

Top: Moise, Etta, Nell, and Sam, at their joint 50th wedding anniversary, 1959 /
Bottom (top): Pauline, Leonard, Melvin, Pearle, Lolita, Lazar, Buddy, Anne,
Helen, and Marvin (holding Marcy); (seated) Moise, Etta, Nell, and Sam;
(bottom) Roslyn, Edward, Janice, Gary, Harriet, Debbie, and Marilyn

Top (seated): Rabbi Perry E. Nussbaum; (to his left) Marilyn; (to his right) Roslyn; (to her right) Edward, in their Beth Israel confirmation class, 1963 / Bottom: Moise and Sam, with Jack, the horse they won at the state fair, c. 1912
FACING PAGE: Top: Sam, Moise, and Etta, Cohen Brothers, 1922 / Center: Leonard, Mrs. Clark (a seamstress), and Lazar, Cohen Brothers, 1946 / Bottom: Leonard, Will Jones, Marguerite Tillman, and Lazar, Cohen Brothers, 1972

Top left: Edward as a southern Jew, Murrah High School, 1966 / Top right: Edward (Eddie) as a northern Jew, University of Miami, 1968 / Bottom: Edward, no longer a *shaygitz*, ETV, 1972

not only never asked but never even seen. Thirty minutes in, the thermostat, the only functioning part of the air-conditioning system, read ninety-five. We had no electric fans, having scorned them as relics as outmoded as wood stoves and given them to the Sisterhood Bazaar. Uncle Sig kept on his suit coat, but everyone else was in shirtsleeves. I could look down and see the outline of my stomach as my shirt clung stickily to my body.

As I did at temple, I surreptitiously thumbed through to the end of the service, as distant as heaven. Janice and Roslyn began muttering loudly to their parents, threatening to leave or scream or both, when Uncle Sig suddenly interrupted his Hebrew reading and silenced them utterly with a fiery burst of Yiddish. The only word I understood was "*wilde.*"

The service continued thereafter uninterrupted. Not one page was skipped. When the meal was finally served, no one but Uncle Sig had any appetite, because of the heat and because of the knowledge that another sixty-eight pages of postprandial service remained.

With our cursory religious observances, we Mississippi Jews must have seemed to other Jews so distant from the ancient faith that we were virtually goyim. Yet to ourselves and to the Christians all around us, we remained unbreachably separate. For some, this isolation was a point of pride, a central element of personal identity. For others it was unbearable.

In our household, conversion to Christianity was considered shameful. From the time I was young, whenever anyone converted they seemed to me to be lost forever. I began to realize how central my Jewishness was to my identity when I came into contact with converts who had, it seemed, willingly given theirs up.

With conversion, one's past was annihilated. One of my

mother's special friends, one of the few she had, converted along with her husband and children. The news ricocheted through the congregation. It seemed as fundamental a change as death. As a child I'd seen her many times playing canasta with all the rest of the Beth Israel ladies, but afterward she quit coming, and eventually her friendship with my mother faded. It was remarkable how quickly she vanished.

A high school friend, whose mother had converted to Christianity when she married, had an old immigrant grandmother who lived with them and spoke with the same accent as my grandparents. She brightened when she heard my last name, asked me hungrily about members of the temple she had once known but now never saw. Then she retreated into her room, a small bent-over creature, stranded not only on the far reach of a distant shore but now regarded by her children and grandchildren as a vestige of a history that was intentionally being forgotten.

I wondered if, as my mother's former friend grew older, she felt stranded and dislocated, like that ancient grandmother who had grasped me like a lifeboat to her past.

Years later, when I was about to marry outside the faith, my mother fatalistically assumed the worst. "If you're going to convert," she said, "do me the kindness of waiting until I'm dead." What a Jewish request!

Conversion to Christianity was inconceivable to me, but what I found even more difficult to grasp was why anyone would want to become one of us. Typically, the reason was marriage to a Jewish spouse. Unlike the proselytizing Christian faiths, however, Judaism discouraged conversion. The converts would be renouncing Christ as their savior—there was no getting around that—and in so doing would be unmooring themselves from the central pivot of their southern world. Those who persisted had to undergo a rigorous program of studies with the rabbi, learning Jewish history and practice, all the while being stringently questioned to ascertain the seriousness of their intention.

Those who emerged from this trial-by-rabbi knew far more about our faith than the average laggard Beth Israel member. With typical convert's zeal they rose to high positions in the temple, and I felt pride, along with continuing amazement, that these gentile-looking men and women with their unimpeachably Anglo-Saxon names were now part of our family.

Jackson, Mississippi, was definitely a hardship post for a rabbi. Beth Israel was not only a small congregation, but it was also located in the state that to northerners was the quintessence of intolerance. Even if a young rabbi graduating from seminary at Hebrew Union College in Cincinnati had a misguidedly adventurous spirit, he had his protesting wife and children to consider. After the gemutlich Jewish nest of seminary, it would have seemed like voyaging out to minister to savages who spoke the same tongue but virtually unintelligibly, who held beliefs that were the same but were recognizable only in broad outline, and who stretched the outside limits of the elastic question "What is a Jew?"

Many were called to Jackson. Few came. The top graduates went to serve as assistants in large temples in New York, Philadelphia, or Los Angeles, where they were surrounded by Jews, bulwarked by Jews, utterly secure in a sustaining womb of Jewishness. Interface with the Christian world could be infrequent, brief, and always a matter of choice. Rabbis who came to Beth Israel needed a job. They could not afford to be choosy.

The ones who survived longest were themselves southern, or else from a culturally neutral place like the Midwest, where, as in the South, the dominant ethos was unalloyedly Christian. Any who ventured from the Northeast soon withered.

The rabbi during my early childhood was a kind-faced man who looked like a Jewish Eisenhower. Meyer Lovitt, who appeared elderly even when he was young, was the perfect rabbi for the early 1950s—inoffensive, nonconfrontational, as easygoing as my grandfather Moise and with as few intellectual pretensions. I do not know if he was southern by birth, but he was by temperament, and he would've stayed forever as rabbi, presiding absently over a somnolent congregation, had he not grown too old to fulfill even the minimal requirements of his duties.

In the early 1970s Beth Israel attracted a more energetic rabbi, not long out of Hebrew Union College, a Memphis resident. Memphis, as described by my father, was just a big Jackson, and the rabbi suffered no cultural dislocation in Mississippi. He was a small, earnest-eyed man with a moustache and a helmet of longish dark hair. He took his duties seriously, as I found when I visited his office one afternoon and told him I was going to get married.

He smiled. "I thought that was what this was about."

"She's not Jewish." His smile vanished.

"I was afraid of that." He sat down behind his desk, putting a barrier between us.

I had undergone several difficult discussions with my Baptist fiance, who wanted a big church wedding. She couldn't understand that I felt threatened and somehow disloyal every time I even stepped inside a church. To me, churches were the seat of otherness, strange places with mysterious rituals and forbidden symbols—the antithesis of a safe house. She opposed having the ceremony in a secular setting and reluctantly agreed to be married in the temple. As for me, the temple in which I had been raised, of which my father had been president, and which my grandfather had attended since the last century, would be as right, as comfortable, as familiar as being married at home.

"Both parties," the rabbi explained, "must be Jewish for

the service to be performed in the temple." I had always thought of the temple as open and receiving. Didn't they ecumenically welcome all on Friday night? Wasn't it a tradition to invite strangers to share the Passover feast "because ye had been strangers in the land of Egypt"?

"As for mixed marriages, I don't perform them," he said with military brevity, "anywhere." I could hear wrapping-up tones in his voice as he stood, though we'd just sat down. He added that he'd heard that the rabbi in Vicksburg might perform them.

Somehow I found myself out the door, without any offer of help in contacting the potentially wavering Vicksburg rabbi or anyone else. I had been maritally excommunicated. After my rabbi's rejection, I had little basis on which to argue against the church wedding. The Baptist preacher was welcoming, cooperative, willing to leave out all references to Jesus in the service. In fact, if I wished to write my own service, he'd be happy to perform it and encouraged me to incorporate Jewish elements into it such as the breaking of the wine glass. I spent hours with him as opposed to minutes with my own rabbi.

My mother excoriated the rabbi. "You're worried about losing Jews to intermarriage," she said one night after temple when she waylaid him on the way to the pastry table, "but you're alienating every Jew who marries a Christian. Open your eyes, Rabbi," she insisted. "We're surrounded by Christians. People have to marry somebody. Wouldn't it be better to welcome them, as the Christians do, instead of pushing them into their arms?"

The rabbi had no argument. He had chosen an all-or-nothing policy and, Vietnam War-like, he was going down with it, no matter how many casualties, reported and unreported, the faith suffered along the way.

Years later, I found myself in the same office but with a different rabbi and a different fiancé. This rabbi was a thick-set young man with a neatly trimmed beard. He and his wife were from a predominantly Jewish neighborhood in the Northeast. Though nominally Reform, they kept kosher and he wore a yarmulke.

This rabbi could never adjust to the South. His wife was accustomed to tiny urban grocery stores, and the sheer sweep of shopping center supergroceries gave her agoraphobia. Most importantly, they were used to being surrounded by a virtually unalloyed population of Jews. Suddenly, the only place they could hope to find a Jew was in the temple, and even there gentiles had infiltrated the janitorial and secretarial ranks. His secretary answered the phone in honeyed southern tones.

"Beth Iz-reel" was what his New York friends heard when they called their wandering friend. The rabbi had come seeking adventure. All he found was dislocation. There was no place to buy the kosher foodstuffs that were essential to him. Even worse, he was starving culturally. Though his tenure was short, he did not leave without the opportunity to marry me.

By the time my second fiance and I approached him, he had heard of the previous rabbi's experience with me and particularly with my mother, and had prepared what he thought would be an effective yet inoffensive refusal.

"The only problem I have with marrying you," he said, forcing some measure of geniality onto his face, "is that the Jewish service requires allegiance to the laws of Moses, and it wouldn't be fair to ask your Christian fiance to do that."

"I wouldn't have a problem with that," Kathy responded instantly.

"But it wouldn't be fair to you."

"I don't mind."

"Then that's all there is to it," I said, wrapping up (by this time I'd been trained as a lawyer).

The rabbi, always a stiff man, became positively rigid.

The truth came out. He didn't approve, it was diluting the faith—all the old rabbi's chestnuts. The rabbi spent what must have been some of the most uncomfortable minutes of his excruciating sojourn in Mississippi listening to me vent my frustration with a faith that not once, but twice, would turn me away to seek solace among the Christians the rabbis were trying so diligently to keep us away from.

Again I was married by a Christian clergyman, this time in the backyard of our house. Again the service was strictly non-Christian (though the Episcopal minister had to physically restrain himself from the habit of making the sign of the cross).

The congregation was more welcoming to Kathy than the rabbi had been. She joined the Temple Sisterhood (being Christian was no impediment), was invited to join Hadassah, the ladies' organization for the support of Israel, and at the temple bazaar would dip up stuffed cabbage, kugle, brisket and carrot tzimmes for her fellow southerners, who waited all year for some real Jewish cooking.

Soon the rabbi was gone, back up north, into his all-Jewish universe. His adventure into the provinces of southern Jewry would probably provide him with tales to tell his grandchildren on scary stormy nights.

Except for the issue of marriage, the rabbis of my adulthood left little impression on me. That could not be said for Perry E. Nussbaum, with whom I was locked in theological combat for most of my youth.

Rabbi Nussbaum had a thin face dominated by a high-bridged, deeply hooked nose and punctuated with a tightly clipped moustache. He retained only a fringe of grayish hair, cropped mercilessly short. His forehead appeared to rise and rise forever over small, impatient eyes drained of any imagined warmth by the sharp glint of his rimless glasses. His voice left the greatest impression: a flat yet piercing nasality, which seemed to originate high in that forehead, concentrated itself in the curve of his nose to emerge like a poison dart from under that little moustache. That voice somehow made everything he said both unpalatable and inarguable.

That voice was not southern. After the complacent Ike-like Rabbi Lovitt, Rabbi Nussbaum was as great a shock to the congregation as if we had all suddenly been sent to a Jewish military school. Rabbi Nussbaum was originally from Canada and had previously served at several congregations for very brief tenures. His passion for Judaism was never disputed, but the prevailing sentiment was that it would have been better for all concerned if he had spent his life in solitary Talmudic exegesis. He was one of those unfortunate people who had no concept of the impression he was making, a situation exacerbated in his case by the fact that he cared very little anyway. In his words and deeds, he took northern brusqueness, abraded it to a bludgeon, and whetted it to a scalpel. He was seldom liked, often despised, yet always respected for his formidable intelligence, encyclopedic learning, and outspoken courage at a time when most Mississippi Jews remained silent.

My earliest clash with the rabbi, over the Passover egg, occurred when I was nine. Hard-boiled eggs had always been one of those foods that I could not bring myself to touch, let alone eat. It was a question of texture, something in that slick rubbery exterior and the too-neat way it separated from its crumbly yellow heart that told me instinctively that my system would revolt if invaded by it. One night my father placed a ten-dollar bill on the breakfast room table alongside a hard-boiled egg. For a small boy in the 1950s, even one whose parents were almost absurdly generous, this was a great deal of money. I stared at those two antipodal entities, one green and crisp, the other white and gleaming, and I walked away.

Rabbi Nussbaum's Passover seder for the Sunday school

children was part of his general shaping-up of the congregation. Since his arrival, the class curriculum had become more exacting and the discipline tighter; the rabbi was demanding that we bring our Jewish knowledge and practices up from a feudal southern level. In the space of a few years we were all being wrenched from a comfortable and laggardly Dark Ages of Jewish practice into a terrible Industrial Revolution of strictures and observance.

At two long tables in the social area of the temple sat every Jewish child in Jackson. Pharaoh could have used the occasion to wipe us out, but in his place was Rabbi Nussbaum.

Each table held several large plates on which the Passover symbols were arrayed. The best was haroset, an exotic mixture of chopped apples, cinnamon, and honey, which symbolized the sweetness of deliverance. I looked forward to it every year at our pre-Uncle Sig, southern-style seders. The haroset I saw before me at the temple that day was a mass-produced institutional version.

Around the bowl of haroset were other symbols, such as bitter herbs for the harshness of slavery and matzo for the unleavened bread the Hebrews hurriedly baked. The hard-boiled egg, the symbolism of which I didn't want to know, was staring at me.

Rabbi Nussbaum directed each child to eat a hard-boiled egg. Obediently every other child did. When the rabbi saw that my hard-boiled egg still sat on my plate, at the far edge so I couldn't smell it, he came and stood behind me.

"Eat the egg, Edward."

"I don't like them."

To Rabbi Nussbaum, my refusal was a sacrilege. Worse, it was a challenge to his authority from a small-for-his-age nine-year-old child.

"If you don't eat the egg, you must leave the Passover seder." The rabbi stared at me, impatient, ready to continue his detailed but largely unheard and totally uncomprehended explanation of some arcane aspect of the service. I stared at the egg.

The table grew quiet at the showdown. The adult Sunday school teachers watched the spectacle in amazement and horror. The seder was the very symbol of welcome and Jewish inclusiveness; even relatives who were never spoken about or to were called home to share the seder. To cast a fellow Jew from the Passover table was unthinkable, especially if the excommunicant was a small child.

The egg glistened, white as a slug under a rock. The look on the rabbi's face was superior, confident; to him, this was a battle not only well worth fighting but one he was sure to win. I stood and walked out. The rabbi stared after me. The battle line had been drawn for the rest of our years together. Adam was cast from Eden for eating the apple of knowledge, I for not eating the egg of obedience.

I went alone into the hallway, unsure of what to do. It was like being the only one absent from Boyd School, except that now I was exiled from the exiles. Surely someone would come and ask me back to the table. No one did. Finally, I asked the maid if I could use the phone and called my father to pick me up.

My father, Tiger, tracked the rabbi to his home. He would have hit him except that Nussbaum, sorry emissary though he was, stood for Judaism in our town. The rabbi shrugged through his impenetrable cuticle of incomprehension.

"Don't make a federal case out of it," he said, with the same approach to human affairs that would soon threaten the survival of his rabbinate in Jackson.

A year later, at Halloween, Rabbi Nussbaum issued an ex cathedra directive that all Beth Israel children were to trick-or-treat for UNICEF, a United Nations relief organization. The rabbi thought it an excellent idea that, instead of receiving useless candy that we would merely enjoy, we could ask for pennies for the U.N.

The United Nations was regarded in Mississippi as, at best, a communist lesion on the country's independence, at worst as the nesting place of Satan. If there could be anything more likely to rile my neighbors than liberal Yankees, it was one-worlders, who would subjugate Christian America to the heathen practices of all those unpronounceable nations whose delegates wore bathrobes in the street.

Such was the political climate when I set out, wearing my mouse costume, into the heart of John Birch-era Mississippi. Instead of a capacious sack to hold Baby Ruths and mints and salt water taffy from the fair, I carried a little cardboard box supplied by the rabbi and emblazoned in easily readable letters with "U.N."

I was not afraid as I knocked on the first door, only monumentally disappointed that every iota of fun had been leeched out of one of my favorite days of the year.

"Trick-or-treat for UNICEF," I piped, thrusting my U.N.-blue box forward. The nice lady's smile curdled and she slammed the door. At some houses I was treated to a lecture on the evils of the U.N. Others in the neighborhood were polite but kept their pennies for less-charged uses. I cut short my trick-or-treat route radically and returned home after less than an hour with perhaps four cents in my box, given by kindhearted neighbors moved by pity. My mother fished around in her purse and came up with thirty-seven more pennies so I would have a respectable showing. When I turned in my box the next Sunday, I learned that my fellow internationalists had encountered the same resistance. The next year the rabbi proposed we march out again with our blue boxes, but, this time backed by our parents, we all simply refused.

When I was fifteen and it came time for me to be confirmed, our Sunday school class was taught for the entire year by Rabbi Nussbaum. We were also required to meet in his office several afternoons a week after school for additional instruction, a further test of our resilience. There we gathered, eight of us, like mice in a cobra's cage.

I'm sure the Count of Monte Cristo could have described every crack in his dank cell. I remember Rabbi Nussbaum's huge cluttered desk with him perched behind it, bald as a malevolent egg. The room was lined with books, dense tracts he would often assign us to read. He would be furious when no one would read them or when I would make heterodox arguments against them. We were like thick stubborn southern mules whose misfortune it was to fall under the management of a northern reformer out to turn us into Jewish racehorses. Cousin Buddy, who taught a class in the room next door, would cup his ear to the wall to listen as I posed unanswerable theological arguments that infuriated the rabbi. At one point, frustrated at the lack of enthusiasm his teaching had engendered, Rabbi Nussbaum demanded a show of hands.

"How many of you are looking forward to my confirmation blessing?"

One by one, hypocritically, the other members of the class raised their hands. Finally it was only Roslyn and I with our hands defiantly down. He stared at us for a long time, perhaps thinking that we would repent. Finally it became even more embarrassing for him than for us, and he moved on.

For me Rabbi Nussbaum was the embodiment of all the restraints and strictures and tiny outrages I'd felt my entire childhood—the stigmata of Marie Hull's magnolias, the inescapable school prayers. Yet here it came in the form of a fellow Jew, someone from my world with whom I was allowed to join battle. I could say things I could never voice in the outer Christian world. Debate, even rancorous argument, was encouraged in Judaism. As infuriating as my questions were, he never cut them off with an authoritarian "because it's in the Bible," as might have ended debate in Christian churches. Not that I ever won or even made a point, but I was heard. I asked, "Didn't one of the Pharaohs come up with the idea of one God before we did?" Or, "What if everybody else was right and Jesus *was* the messiah?" And, of course, "If we're God's Chosen People, why does he let so many bad things happen to us?"

Sometimes, he'd reward my persistence with an additional assignment in one of those thick Judaic tracts. They slowed me some—the treatises were incomprehensible to a fifteen-year-old—but I swallowed as much of them as I could so I could rejoin the fray the next Sunday. Once he assigned me an essay on the topic "The Mediocrity of Sunday-school Students," and I responded with a broadside arguing that our deficiency was in direct proportion to the mediocrity of the instructor. He never commented on it, but from the edge in his voice the next Sunday I knew he had read it.

Rabbi Nussbaum's northern contentiousness was not limited to the Sunday school, and he had been in Jackson only a few years when a faction of the congregation began to plot actively for his dismissal. Insurrection was not in character for our sleepy congregation. Rabbi Lovett, the previous rabbi, had dozed through decades at the helm, but he did not possess Rabbi Nussbaum's uncanny ability to offend.

The militant faction of the congregation circulated a petition demanding that Nussbaum be fired, and a sizable number of members signed it. The petition posed two problems for the congregation. First, how would we ever get another rabbi to come to godforsaken Jackson, Mississippi? It had been hard enough to get even Nussbaum. Then, there were the legal and moral issues—he had just signed a new contract. The temple split into two warring factions. Opposing the militants was a loyalist minority, for whom the office of rabbi, no matter how occupied, demanded respect. The militants grew in strength; more and more members signed the petition.

My father was president of the congregation during this civil war, and, like Lincoln, he was obliged to stand for union. He had to ignore all the history between the rabbi and me and fight for Nussbaum during the most critical test to date for the Beth Israel congregation. At Friday night services, at the store, late at night on the phone, the militants tried to wear my father down. As president, he wielded moral power, and, had he switched sides, it is certain that Nussbaum would have been the Andrew Johnson of Jewry, the first rabbi to be in effect impeached.

My father proved to be a brilliant tactician, something I never would've guessed. The uprising was, after all, nothing more than the inter-Cohen wars of Fortification Street, much expanded into the entire Jewish family of Jackson. He knew the militants had the force of numbers and momentum, while his strength lay in the static power of the institution of the temple and its constitution. My father simply waited them out, enduring the months of acrimony and vilification until the militants' passion finally spent itself against the walls of the status quo, while he quietly picked up support. In the end, Nussbaum remained at the pulpit. Though a few members resigned from the congregation, the union was preserved. For saving his hide, Rabbi Nussbaum gave my father a very qualified thank you. It was all he was capable of.

Perry Nussbaum remained in office, to lead Beth Israel into the coming civil rights years, when his unpopular and outspoken views would put the congregation directly in the path of the collision between North and South.

The Store

"The same people who say 'nigger' are going to say 'kike.'"
My remonstrance to a fellow southern Jew during the civil rights years

"Are there Jews here?"
A *shnorrer* (Jewish beggar), stopping by for a handout

Cohen Brothers was my Big House. From the time of my earliest memories until I was well into adulthood, it was a place I was always welcome, where family could always be found. No matter how many times I might move, the store was a constant; lost letters caught up with me there, as did long-forgotten friends who were passing through. If I needed a place to park downtown, if I ran short of money and the banks were closed, if I needed an emergency tailoring job for a crucial date, the store never failed me. I knew how much I valued having this second home while the store was open. I didn't know how badly I would miss it when it finally closed.

Cohen Brothers was a perpetual family reunion, Sundays-at-Granny's the other six days of the week. Though retired, Moise and Sam would spend half-days there to greet old friends. My father and Lazar constituted the main sales force, along with Uncle Melvin, while Aunt Pearle did the books. During the Christmas rush, the reserves would be called in: my mother, Lolita, Gary, and I to sell, Roslyn to staff the gift-wrap table. When I was growing up, five Cohen families—fourteen people in all—derived their income from Moise and Sam's immigrant beachhead, the *shtorke* (unassuming little store, pronounced shtork'-ee) at 224 West Capitol Street.

From the time I was twelve, I spent most Saturdays and much of my Christmas vacation working at the store. I started out with simple sales—caps and ties—then, as I grew older, mastered shirts and hats, and, finally, once it had been ascertained I could wield a measuring tape and marking chalk, graduated to pants and suits. At first I couldn't reach the handle of the 1900-vintage National cash register, so, when I made a sale, I would call out, "Cash sale," and my father or Lazar would ring it up and make change. Even as an adult, I never mastered the intricacies of the charge or lay-away systems, which involved an on-the-spot determination of creditworthiness often based on a decades-long association with the customer.

I was not a natural salesman like my father. He could work up a genuine enthusiasm that spread to the customer, so that a suit would lead inevitably to hats, shoes, and a shirt plus three ties thrown in for free, all piled up on the same oak table on which Ike Levy had displayed his swatches to Moise and Sam. By contrast, I showed the customer only what he asked for, unsparked by the combat of sales, never grasping the connection between what went into the cash register and how many special-ordered strip sirloins from New York were served on Brook Drive.

I enjoyed the lulls in business, when I could read my book or write, but my father would stare through the glass front door out onto Capitol Street, watching the window shoppers, hoping they'd be tempted in. On really bad days, when I got a lot of writing done, and Aunt Pearle would finish an entire mystery novel sitting in the shoe department, and Lazar brought all the credit ledgers up to date, my father would range up Capitol Street like a guerilla scout, descrying where the crowds were and if they were moving in the direction of the store. Those were the days when Gary and I could take long lunch breaks at Odis' Barbeque to confer on pressing stamp matters.

Two hours later Gary and I would return through the back door to a store full of customers, with my father and Lazar waiting on three people at once while Pearle furiously scribbled down charges. My father would yell, "Front! Front! Store full of customers!" and Gary and I would wade in where the crowd was thickest.

Often there might be fifty shoppers and nine Cohen family members crammed into what could generously be called a modest space. The storefront measured at most fifteen feet across, and the black-and-white tiled floors reached back perhaps sixty feet deep. The tin ceiling was enormously high, at least twenty feet, with two skylights reaching another twenty feet to the roof, enough room for all the gods and goddesses of Greek and Roman mythology to look down upon our scurrying commerce.

All the fixtures were antique, not by design but because they had not been modernized after two world wars. Though the display cases were mahogany, as was all the shelving, the rich wood had been painted a fleshy tan in an ill-advised effort during the 1950s to "lighten" the mood and keep up with the times. At the back of the store was an office, utterly open to the rest of the store, separated only by a low wall topped with glass and two sets of prison-like bars where money was exchanged between customer and Cohen.

The small office was crowded with what I, an archivist even at twelve, saw as memorabilia-in-the-making. On the walls were photos depicting the various geological ages of Cohen history: Moise and Sam as green immigrants, looking dignified and hopeful; Jack, the horse Sam had won, pulling a surrey; World War II photos of Leonard, Lazar, Buddy, and Marvin; an inexpertly glassined newspaper clipping of the old folks' double fiftieth wedding anniversary party. Beneath these ancient Lascaux-like images were flesh-tan painted shelves, bent with giant twenty-pound ledgers containing the handwritten payment history of our customers. Most sales were on credit and had been since the first day the store opened; that their black clientele had little cash was something the immigrants understood from their own experience.

The ledgers would be lifted to the desk and consulted

like the Talmud to determine if a suit could be charged to an account and how much money down was necessary. A person's entire life, economic and emotional, could be divined from the cramped entries in Lazar's fine calligraphic notes or my father's more hurried jottings: "Late with payment, lost job, daughter sick," followed later by "suit for funeral, will pay $20 by 1st."

The phone sat in the middle ground between the store floor and the office, so that customers or Cohens were equally likely to be using it—a customer asking for a ride or gauging the correct size for a gift, my father calling to make sure my mother was okay, Lazar being informed by Lolita of the evening's social plans. I often cursed the lack of privacy, particularly during my teen years when I tried to sneak in a romantic call between measuring a crotch and ringing up a sock sale.

Just outside the office, to one side, was a minuscule alcove grandly called the shoe department, where sometimes Melvin, Lazar, and my father might be simultaneously mounted like unlikely jockeys on shoe stools as they maneuvered Freeman and Stacy-Adams shoes onto six feet. On these occasions Aunt Pearle would be displaced from her Perry Mason library.

Excepting the ever-mounting layers of flesh-tan enamel, little changed in the store's appearance over the decades. Old photographs reveal the never-altering placement of display cases and hat boxes dating back to when Moise and Sam had pooled peddling money to build the store in 1898.

Lazar and my father started working Saturdays and Christmas holidays as they entered their teens (just as Gary and I would do a half-century later). It was the Cohen version of bar mitzvah, of becoming an adult.

At lunchtime, the store would close, and Moise, Sam, Leonard, and Lazar would ride back to the Big House for lunch, where, just as at supper, Moise prohibited business talk, even during the Depression when the store almost went bankrupt. Amidst the slurping of gumbo or matzo ball soup, the silences of pent-up but unaskable questions must have been unendurable to the rest of the family, whose often-precarious livelihood depended on the *shtorke.* One day they returned from lunch to find an agent of the power company waiting to cut off their lights. He told Moise that the utility had carried him longer than Moise's own mother. My father, Tiger, stopped the agent at the door, saying he'd have to go through him. The lights remained on.

As the country pulled out of the Depression and my father and Lazar grew to adulthood in the store, they came into increasing conflict with their fathers. Leonard and Lazar had ambitions—to get better brands, to advertise, to modernize. Moise and Sam, aging patriarchs who were satisfied with survival, were unyielding. They'd taken enough risks, leaving Romania, then coming south, surviving the Klan's resurgence in the 1920s, being dunned by bill collectors throughout the next decade. The battle would rage all day at the store, with a forced truce every night once the four pulled into the driveway at the Big House.

World War II interrupted the conflict. Leonard and Lazar went to India and Italy, respectively, leaving their fathers, both now approaching seventy, to run the store. By the time Leonard and Lazar returned from the war, the patriarchs' conservatism had resulted in a store virtually empty of merchandise and, perforce, of customers.

My father, just back from Asia, went on a mad cross-country buying trip by Pullman to New Orleans, then Atlanta, then New York, where he wheedled, begged, and argued with every wholesale clothes jobber who would listen to him and extend credit. Despite the postwar scarcity of any kind of merchandise, giant packages soon started arriving at Cohen Brothers—hats, suits, shoes, some of them brand names. Leonard the gambler ran his credit line as far as he could talk it, and the postwar customers, flush with the times, flocked in to buy the store bare, sometimes before the merchandise had been uncrated. The moribund ladies' department was swept out with the need for floor space, and, within the black community, Cohen Brothers became the leading men's clothier in Jackson. Moise and Sam were happy to ease into semiretirement, which meant sitting all day in the shoe department.

A few customers still brought them to their feet. When a band of Gypsies would enter, speaking their native tongue, Romany, Sam would go to the front. They were unaware that he, like them, was from Romania and knew their language. If they were making plans to steal, it would take only a few sentences from him in Romany to convince them to seek another mark. And often any of a number of old white farmers, in town with their grandchildren, would seek out Cohen Brothers for a talk with "Morris" the peddler, who had slept in the hayloft a half-century before.

The store also attracted *schnorrers*, Jewish beggars drawn unerringly by the name "Cohen." The *schnorrers* seemed an oddity because all the Jews from the temple were, or at least seemed to be, prosperous. Most were merchants; others were doctors or lawyers or scrap dealers. Unlike the North, the South had few poor or even blue-collar Jews. Perhaps the tenacity required for going the extra thousand miles south ensured some measure of success.

Success had eluded the *schnorrers*. In their appearance they were no different from other "bums" of the time: unshaven, dirty, wearing rags. Yet beneath their battered hats and unwashed curls was an unquestionably Jewish face, often an intelligent one, and the older ones spoke in the same accent as my grandparents. I had somehow thought that being Jewish, with its strong family tradition and emphasis on education, was an inoculation against utter failure, but the *schnorrers* were a discomforting refutation of my notions of Jewish superiority. I watched as my father or Lazar listened to their stories; the visitors always seemed at pains to convince them that they were Jewish. Then my father gave them money and a hat for the summer sun, a sweater if it was cold.

During the Depression, Granny always gave sandwiches to indigents, irrespective of religion, and on the sidewalk in front of the Big House was scraped a circle with an arrow, which said in the secret language of the needy that this house would feed them. Though the store had no arrow out front, I'm certain that its verbal equivalent was passed along the *schnorrer* network.

I can only guess at how being Jewish would have added to the problems of a travelling bum in the South. Their gentile peers wouldn't have had the fine tactfulness of the Christians of my acquaintance. However, the *schnorrers* had one advantage: a bond that would never fail them.

When I was growing up, downtown was still the center of commerce in Jackson. Capitol Street was a raucous thriving place, its sidewalks full on Saturdays with blacks and whites in almost equal measure.

Inside most establishments the races parted. There was never any question but that the three hotels on Capitol Street—the Walthall, the Heidelberg, and the King Edward—allowed only white guests, or that the Greek restaurants—Primos, the Elite, the Mayflower, People's Cafe—didn't serve blacks. Of course, all these businesses were staffed by blacks, from the ancient man who swept up hair clippings at the King Edward barbershop to the stooped operator in the claustrophobic Heidelberg elevators with the sign "Yes we're small but aren't we fast?" to the spittoon emptiers at the Walthall. This stark divide never seemed odd to me as a child, since it was the way everything was and always had been.

Farther down the street were the grandest of the white-only downtown movie theatres, the Paramount and, just off Capitol Street, the Lamar. Both had enormous balconies, deco-era decadent gilt walls, and velveteen seats. I watched *Gone with the Wind* from high in the Paramount balcony, surrounded by a sea of white faces as rapt as my own.

Black theatres such as the Amite were far less grand. As I rode past these theatres every Saturday on my way to the store, I could see that everything about them seemed slightly run-down, faded—from the cracked glass over the movie posters to the missing letters on the marquee to the half-burned-out neon sign. I preferred the Paramount, where everything gleamed with the sparkle that only money could impart.

Across the street from the Paramount were the dime stores, Woolworth's and Kress, where whites and blacks roamed the aisles together but parted abruptly at the lunch counter, where blacks were not allowed, except as cooks.

One restaurant where there was severely circumscribed integration was the Krystal, just a short block from the store. The Krystal served a tiny ten-cent square hamburger with grilled onions and mustard on a grease-moist square bun. I'd seen high school girls gorge eight at a sitting and real trenchermen sixteen. The restaurant, like its hamburgers, was miniature, exactly the size of an Oldsmobile, as I learned when the building was torn down to make a parking lot. The high school girls, the trenchermen, and I would balance on red stools, devouring the three-bite burgers and never dreaming that this taste would be the one we would remember, idealize and long for, when our digestive systems, palates, and good sense would no longer allow the indulgence. While we sat, sometimes a black person would enter, stand to the side near the wall and place an order to go, then take his morsel from the white world around the corner to some private place.

Of the black restaurants and stores up and down Farish Street near the store, I knew nothing. They were as alien and forbidding to me as a Christian church.

But the one-block radius around the store was literally as familiar to me as my own backyard and is imbedded as deeply in my memory. One of my earliest recollections of Capitol Street—I must have been no more than five—was of being deposited at the State Theatre across the street from the store for a double feature. It would've been during the Christmas rush, when my mother was pressed into service and needed a nearby place where I'd be happy and out of the way.

Although it was perfectly safe there in the early 1950s, for me that vast dark room, mostly empty except for a few strangers, was terrifying. By the time the second feature started, I'd lost any sense of time and began to fear I'd been left there forever. I went out into the brightly lit lobby but I couldn't see Cohen Brothers, so I went back and huddled in the dark alone, while on the screen mad horses careened and huge cowboys grimaced as in a nightmare. When finally (it had actually been less than three hours) my mother came for me, she didn't know why I grasped her hand so tightly or why my face was bathed in relief as we crossed Capitol Street and I looked through Cohen Brothers' glass door at the bustling business and the flesh-tan tables and my father, reassuringly and unmistakably real under the fluorescent lights.

As I grew older, I explored the area around the store, just as a country boy would map nearby creeks and woods. There were a few fine establishments, surviving from the era when being near the train station meant something. Just across the street was the mighty King Edward Hotel (not the shameful ruin it is now), where legislators still gathered and

Uncle Melvin slept his lunch hour away in the lobby with a newspaper over his face. Adjacent was the coffee shop, where my mother and I might have lunch with my father on a weekday when business was slack, though he was always glancing across the street, worried that he might see a wave of customers sweep into the store and inundate Lazar. A couple of doors down was Bourgeois Jewellers, a daunting place where two regal and antique sisters presided over a kingdom of towering carved mahogany cases, none painted flesh-tan.

Mostly what I encountered on my explorations outside the store was the underside of downtown Jackson. When the store closed for the day, and light was failing, we'd exit through the back, then clang heavy metal doors into place. We had a small unpaved parking area and a collapsing sheet-metal garage that dated from when Moise and Sam first built the store. An unsteady gunmetal gray staircase led to the top floor of the store, which we rented out to an establishment known as the Capitol Hotel. When, as a teenager, I asked my father what went on up there, he explained without embarrassment as we drove back to northeast Jackson that the owner, our tenant, let out rooms by the hour to prostitutes. It was difficult for me to reconcile our perfect middle-class existence with the fact that a virtual whorehouse was in operation above the store. I glimpsed for the first time how tenuous, and recent, was our grip on respectability.

The only way to exit the parking area was through an alleyway less than a foot wider than the car, bordered by two other hotels no more reputable than the Capitol but with which we, mercifully, had no affiliation. The brick walls of the alley were scarred and chipped with three generations of Cohen vehicular miscalculations. Uncle Sam in particular had left his mark, often charging through, banging from wall to wall without stopping until he shot out onto the street.

A few doors down Capitol Street was the poolroom, one of the old-fashioned disreputable unsanitized poolrooms, frequented by, I guessed, the rough men who during the previous night might have climbed the staircase to the Capitol Hotel before retiring in the flophouses that shadowed the alley. I was never comfortable in the poolroom, where my father would sometimes pick up bottles of beer for Moise, Lazar, and himself, and he wasn't totally at ease there either. Despite my father's many southern ways, I sensed that everyone knew we didn't belong.

Moise did feel at home in the pool hall and spent many hours there after he semiretired, drinking beer, telling stories but mostly listening to them. Perhaps the immigrant was the most uncomplicatedly southern of us all.

After a beer, or two, he'd step back onto Capitol Street, blinking behind his round wire-rim glasses in the sudden light, and amble the half-block back to the store, a natty dresser in Panama hat and brown-and-white wing tips, to take his place by his brother Sam and receive visitors in the shoe department.

Cohen Brothers was a gathering spot for blacks, too, as much as a white-owned establishment could be. In the days before shopping centers and black-owned stores, few clothiers in Jackson specifically and solely catered to a black clientele. Church members could count on seeing members of their congregation and their preacher at the store; college students encountered their professors; neighbors visited with neighbors before heading farther up Capitol Street; and proud grandparents of pro football and basketball superstars up north accepted congratulations for their kin's performances and bought sweaters for them at Christmas.

Our merchandise was not expensive. Most suits were $49.95, black or navy for funerals, brown for a second suit, with the iridescent top-of-the-line going for $79.95. Most of our customers worked with their hands—as railroad men, painters, carpenters—and usually a funeral suit was all they needed. But everyone wore hats, straw for summer, felt for winter, starting at $9.95 for the most popular, a Champ bowler hat, and going up to the unimaginable figure of $20.00 for a heavy-felt Knox with a large shady brim. Try as I might, I could never crease those bowler hats the way my father could—a surgical chop down the middle, two quick pinches along the crown, and the bowler would be transformed from fusty to suave.

Almost everything was bought on credit, with a small amount down and even smaller weekly payments. In those days, remembered by me as a period of innocence and affluence, the financial condition of blacks in Mississippi was precarious, untenable. Most black women made their living as maids, earning perhaps twenty dollars a week in the 1950s, their pay often unofficially supplemented by hand-me-downs and leftovers but rarely by bonuses. Many black men held low-paying jobs as handymen, gas station attendants, or yardmen. Although some held jobs in one of Jackson's few factories, there were not many middle-class blacks in Jackson, mostly teachers, preachers, or postal workers.

I would sometimes spend an hour with a customer and would be exultant that I—inept salesman that I was—had racked up a suit, sport coat, and two pairs of shoes, totalling perhaps $125. My celebration was only preliminary, because my sale had to survive the credit negotiations, which were far beyond my competence and fell under the jurisdiction of my father or Lazar. If the customer already had an account, out would come the twenty-pound ledger books. A practiced finger would run down the credit history before arriving at a calculation that was half science and half art. If there had been no late payments in the past, my father might ask for forty dollars down and twenty-five dollars dollars a week. The customer might make a counteroffer, asking for nothing down. Back and forth they'd go, but I knew from my father's comfortable body language—and the customer's, too—that the sale was going to be approved, probably with twenty dollars down and fifteen dollars a week, and that this would be added to the customer's current balance and payments. Other times, though, the customer's and my hopes would sink when an impediment was uncovered in the store's Bible.

"You were a little slow last winter," my father might say. That would mean several payments missed, perhaps several months.

My father might try to get half down so that if the account became uncollectible the store would at least recoup its cost. Often it was simply a gut decision on Leonard's or Lazar's part. My father, the gambler, more often than not would go for the sale, and there would be smiles all around as he instructed me, "Wrap it up, Mr. Cohen."

Sometimes his gut decisions were wrong, and the Magnolia Credit Association would have to be mobilized. Magnolia was a wholly fictitious organization, with the same post office box as the store, operating out of a letter file on top of a table in the store office. The association had five letters that went to slow-paying customers, the first a gentle reminder, then others leading up to Number Five, with its stiffly formal, yet almost wounded tones of regret that legal action would soon follow.

On Christmas Eve, all the negotiations, all the sales, all the phoned credit checks would go into quadruple-time. Despite ourselves, we got into the Christmas spirit. It was impossible not to, so jubilant and excited were the customers who crowded the display cases, waited in line to get into the two dressing rooms, and stood sideways to get past each other to have their purchases rung up and gift-wrapped.

We had little time to go to the bathroom or to eat lunch.

My father would set up sliced meats, breads, cheese, and pickles from the Olde Tyme Delicatessen, and we'd eat in shifts, standing up, washing the food down with a cold beer from the pool hall. I remember the hasty sandwiches as tasting better even than Krystal hamburgers, and the whole ritual—choosing bologna or ham, rye or challah, watching the front door in case I'd suddenly have to leap into the breach, mouth full, beer left behind—is as freighted with tradition and meaning for me as a Passover seder.

Around six o'clock business would suddenly slack off, but we'd be open for another two hours so the alterations could be completed and picked up. About seven o'clock I'd be instructed to pull the shade down over the door, and the store's second seder would begin.

This traditional feast would be more relaxed. The Greek restaurant owners, from the People's Cafe or the Mayflower, would bring down an elaborate plate of stuffed shrimp, olives, and feta cheese, receiving a shirt and tie in return. The Scotch bottle, which had waited in sanctification inside the store's huge pink safe, would be uncapped.

Though people continued filtering into the store to buy last-minute gifts, the revels had begun, as symbolized by the fact that I was allowed to wait on customers with a drink in my hand. Other Capitol Street merchants would swing by for a drink on their way home, and soon the non-Cohen-Brothers Cohens—Buddy and Ann, Marvin and Helen—would come through the front door. By this time it was dark, the metal doors had been swung and locked, and the alleyway and back of the store were now territory occupied by the demimonde of the Capitol Hotel.

Buddy and Marvin, as "professional men"—dentist and lawyer respectively—had little connection with the store, but on the Christmas Eves of my teens, the Big House and Sundays at Granny's would again be replicated, as all waited for the last alteration to be picked up.

Then in a Jewish caravan we'd drive to Crechale's restaurant, an atmospheric vinyl-boothed shrine to the past, with a cult following and legendary onion rings and kum-bak salad dressing, one of the few restaurants open on Christmas Eve. While Christian families in Jackson were caroling, preparing for midnight church, hurriedly wrapping presents to put under the tree or cooking the next day's dinner, our family also gathered together, a travelling outpost of Jewish unity. Gary and I would trade sales anecdotes and compare totals, the Scotch bottle would be replaced by its twin, and everyone looked forward to sleeping through much of Christmas Day.

As a white person, my world was utterly separate from the black half of Jackson, and the lives and sorrows of the people who lived there were unimaginable to me. Yet, because of the store, my life was intertwined with that black world probably more than any other person in my school. As I grew up, two employees of the store were always present, almost family, but always separate, with race an inescapable shadow between us, never mentioned and never forgotten.

In the mid-1920s, when my father and Lazar returned by train from a visit to Uncle Ike in Memphis, a teenage boy their own age, barefoot, with frizzy red hair and freckled skin, reached through the window for their luggage. In a black accent that always surprised coming from that white face, he said, "Mister Moise and Mister Sam sent me." Will Jones became the store's factotum—"porter" was his official title—and his province extended from the sales floor at Cohen Brothers to the sink at the Big House. He was more often called "Red," for the color of his hair—almost the only reminder he had of his white father—or "Cadillac Red" in the black community, courtesy of the store car he'd tear through town in. Red remained at Cohen Brothers for the next sixty years and became probably the only black man in Mississippi with a solid working knowledge of Yiddish curses.

Red's duties were undefined. It was assumed that he could fix anything, though actually his handyman abilities were limited and there was always a chance that the toilet or screen door or drippy faucet might be worse after his ministrations. Red's driving skills rivalled Uncle Sam's. The entrance to the alley was scarred by his miscalculations, each dislodged brick speaking of some ancient collision. Even so, every day he'd chauffeur Moise and Sam back to the Big House for lunch. During World War II, when Moise and Sam were left to run the store, Red had counseled them to return almost all the merchandise they had ordered because, he advised, it wasn't what black people would buy. The old folks' decision to follow his counsel, combined with their growing conservatism, had poised Cohen Brothers on the brink of oblivion by the time the boys returned from the war.

Red's life was intimately commingled with the family's. In 1942, when my father went off to war, it was Will Jones who drove him away from the Big House, while Granny stood on the porch crying, and Will who shook his hand at the train station. As I grew up, the week didn't go by that he didn't appear at Brook Drive one or more times to repair something, as he did at Lazar's house and Pearle's. At the Big House and later on Windermere, Granny would share confidences with him while he tried to fathom her toilet, and he had Moise and Sam's undivided attention every day as he drove them home. After my father and Lazar built black rental houses, he collected rent. The rest of the time, he was on the floor of the store alongside Leonard and Lazar. When his mother died, and later his son, all the Cohens were at the funerals, and, during the years of strict segregation, Red sat with the family at Moise's funeral in 1962 and at Sam's less than a year later.

Red's relationship with the Cohens was always a complicated one. Though he was in our houses nearly every day, we were never once in his, as was typical in black-white relationships of the time. He spent almost every working hour with the family or in their service, yet his loyalties were, had to be, mixed. He was black, and all our family income was derived by commerce with blacks. Sometimes by business necessity, that commerce became adversarial. If the letters from the Magnolia Credit Association were ineffective, my father would have to go to the justice of the peace, who, after taking his fee, would garnish the customer's wages. Some customers were turned down for credit. Some renters had to be evicted. Though the black community in Jackson was large—over fifty thousand during the years I worked in the store—in many ways it was like a small Mississippi town, and throughout that community Will Jones was the emissary of Cohen Brothers.

Like me, Will Jones was torn between two worlds. He was usually friendly and talkative, but the conversations he and I had were wide rather than deep, general not personal—the perversity of the store car, his search for a pipe shaped like a cigar, a funny story about my grandfather. He had a bitter side though, something that could have come from his one-minute meetings with his white father, who came to the store to ask Will for money, or from the divide he spanned between black and white.

To our faces, he disparaged the slow payers, the customers who went bankrupt, the tenants who disappeared owing six months' rent. Behind our backs, as we learned from customers and tenants, he talked about us and told them to shop elsewhere. Twice my father caught him stealing. I learned of these difficulties at the dinner table (at our house we had no embargo on store talk, which often started at breakfast and continued until I went to sleep and, I imagine, pursued my mother into the bedroom and bathroom).

My father for years talked about firing Will but never did it. How do you fire someone as familiar as family, even though the connection is through time and memory instead of by blood and creed? So he remained until he became thin and gray. I found him a pipe shaped like a cigar, but by then his heart was failing and his doctor didn't allow him to smoke. He came in to work on the days when he felt good enough. In the end, long after Moise and Sam were gone, it was just my father and Lazar and Red, old men long past the age of retirement but still standing duty on the store's tiled floor.

I liked Red, but I would have to say that I loved Marguerite Tillman, the store's seamstress. Marguerite was thin, almost frail; she'd had a bout with cancer and lived in fear of its return. Like my mother, she had fine features, but with a dreamer's eyes, and she was possessed of a loony, fatalistic humor. She learned Yiddish, like Red, and was fond of analogies between her life and being "up *sheis* [shit] creek." She'd completed two years of college, extraordinary for a black woman in Mississippi in those years.

It was fortunate that she was small, because what we termed the "Alterations Department" was really a cramped loft-like second floor just above the office, and the ornate tin ceiling was precisely five feet, six inches above the rough planked floorboards. Marguerite and I could walk without bending, but my father, Lazar, and Gary had to scuttle around in a deep stoop.

Marguerite sat all day at an ancient sewing machine, perhaps one of the very first electric models. It was slow, and as she grew older and her fingers stiffened with arthritis, the alterations would back up on the water pipe behind her where the pants and coats hung, one behind the other, like impatient courtiers. My father, hoping to speed up the process, brought in new machines for her to try but she always found something wrong with them. I think she was more comfortable with an early model, like herself. Her work was fastidious, probably better than the quality of the merchandise. Except in a custom tailor, her attention to detail couldn't be found today.

Hard to Marguerite's right in the cramped upstairs was the store's printing press, where Lazar would crank out signs with hopeful but generally futile admonishments such as "No food or drink" and, from the era of double knit when one spark would result in an evil-smelling frizzy hole the size of a nickel, "No smoking in Suit Department." The rest of the upstairs was a forest of suits, the ones left from last season and those constituting "the Layaway Department." In the far corner was a giant upturned toilet paper box that served both as the Cohen Brothers' executive dining room and as the shipping-and-receiving depot of Cohen Stamp Distributors.

During a time in my early teens when I had few friends, Jewish or Christian, and couldn't wait to get out of Mississippi, I spent many afternoons after school upstairs at the store with my stamps and Marguerite. She talked about her health and her money problems, and we concluded we were both quite a distance up *sheis* creek. As she grew to trust me, she gave me her views on the various Cohens, based on how much innate kindness she felt they had, and her perceptions were as fine as her needlework.

When the civil rights movement rolled into the state, Marguerite told me that the outsiders were troublemakers and that she was frightened. Her true thoughts about the matter would always be barred to me, a white, no matter how young I was or how close we might be. Though she was three times my age, she always called me "Mister Edward," and I didn't protest.

She was my friend, for a time even my best friend, but as with Red I never stepped inside her home, only saw it from the outside when we dropped her off after work. The house she rented was shotgun style—one room directly behind the other—with thin curtains and a tattered lawn. She lived with her two sons, one my age, her husband long gone and never mentioned. I'd often see her sons visit her at the store, and as an idealistic teenager imagined that we might be friends. I had no idea how it could be done. Color transcended everything.

One afternoon, after the store closed, Marguerite and I were sitting in the car, waiting for my father after a busy Saturday. I remember precisely where we were, parked on Capitol Street outside a hamburger stand, Tanner's Luncheonette, where whites sat and blacks were allowed to place orders to go; Marguerite often got her lunch there and took it upstairs to eat at her machine. Next door, I could see the poolroom, where I was never comfortable with the rednecks and where no blacks ever went but where Marguerite was often sent to get a beer for my father and Lazar and herself. I imagine it took some courage for her to open the heavy door and order, staying as close to the exit as she could, all the time feeling the stares of the men at the tables. I remember talking to Marguerite about something inconsequential, playing with words, stringing adjectives together, when accidentally, irrevocably, one of those adjectives was "nigger." I stopped. We sat in silence for a moment. I'm certain her awkwardness was even greater than mine. I said, "I'm sorry," and she said, too quickly, "That's all right," but I had damaged something gauzily fine that we'd had between us. The years wove over the tiny rip, and maybe she forgot, but I never did.

After the store closed, I tried to remain in contact with Marguerite, but the store was the institution that had allowed us to bridge the color gap. I sent her a Christmas present every year, money, which she always called to thank me for. When I left Mississippi, I called her. I hadn't talked to her for two or three years and when she came to the phone, her voice was weak, the voice of an eighty-year-old who had never been strong. I told her I was leaving; it was implicit that we'd never speak again.

At the end, impulsively, I said, "I love you."

"I know you do," she said, and it was true, we never spoke again.

My father owned, either solely or in partnership with Lazar or Pearle, approximately twenty rental houses, built from the 1930s to the 1950s when they could borrow the money necessary to construct a simple three- or four-room shotgun house. All the tenants were black.

The houses were basic, barebones. When my father first started building them, during the Depression, two hundred dollars from the bank was sufficient to construct one. All had indoor plumbing, electricity, and gas heating—amenities not universal in Mississippi. They were poverty-level dwellings, for tenants who lived in poverty. In the early 1960s the rent for half a duplex was nine dollars a week, fourteen dollars for a house.

My father was conscientious, even obsessive, about repairs, as he was about any responsibility. If someone called about a broken toilet or heater, sometimes phoning at midnight or two in the morning, my father would lie awake most of the night worrying, and then race to the rental house before the store opened to appraise the situation and determine whether it was within Will Jones's capabilities or whether a real repairman would have to be called. Later he would drive past the house to check the progress of the repair. The forays across town to the house served no purpose except to put him closer to his worry, and my mother would become infuriated when he'd announce right after supper, "I'm just going to drive out to the house on Ash Street," or, more mendaciously but not fooling her, "I'm going to take a drive."

Sometimes on Sunday mornings I would go with him to collect the rent. I was no more than nine, I loved being with my father, and at first it seemed like a grand adventure. Leaving suburbia, with its comfortable ranch houses set back from the street by pine-shaded lawns, we'd drive across town into the other half of Jackson.

There the streets were narrow, often little more than one lane, with the houses hard upon the road. Some houses had porches furnished with faded indoor sofas, some were crumbling and bespoke the landlord's view that they got what they paid for, some had tiny gardens of tomatoes and beans. When we reached one of my father's houses, he parked in front, wrote out a receipt, walked to the door, and exchanged it for crumpled bills and sometimes a handful of change.

One Sunday I asked him to let me go up. He smiled, wrote out the receipt, and instructed me to knock on the door and announce, "Rent man." I walked up the wooden steps, onto the narrow porch. I had never seen the houses up close before. Uncertain now, I knocked on the edge of the screen door, and it rattled in its jamb. No one came, and I wanted to give up. Though my father owned the house, I felt that I didn't belong there. Then the door swung open, revealing a little black girl, no more than five. She stared at me, and I said what I was supposed to say: "Rent man." She didn't smile, and the game was not fun any more.

She disappeared, leaving the door ajar. I didn't want to look inside, to intrude further, but I saw a small cheerless room with old dusty furniture, rickety even when it was made, destined never to be antique, only junk. Though it was a bright day, the sunlight seemed to drown in the room, and there was a hopeless musty smell. It was morning but already hot on the porch and hotter inside. An ancient woman in a faded housedress appeared and handed me nine dollars; I wordlessly gave her the receipt. I wasn't comfortable with the transaction, with being part of it. I thought of our living room with nice carpet and new furniture and our air-conditioning. As we drove to the next house, I felt both enormously guilty and very lucky. Relief at my good fortune—at my not having to live there—was the stronger emotion. I didn't ask to go up to any more of the houses that day, and I didn't ask to go along the next Sunday.

Our maid lived in a house like that, but I didn't think about what I didn't have to see. To my child's mind, she lived on Brook Drive, just as my teachers lived in their Boyd classrooms, and I couldn't conceive of their separate existence.

In Jackson during the 1950s, virtually every white middle-class family had a full-time black maid. At every bus stop in the suburbs around Brook Drive, crowded buses would disgorge black women ranging in age from twenty to seventy but wearing identical starched white uniforms, carrying brown grocery sacks containing personal items—medicine, food, a Bible. On any given afternoon, hundreds, even thousands, of black women in their uniforms could be seen pinning billowing white sheets to clotheslines all over northeast Jackson. Every night, if the maid had stayed past the time the buses ran, the streets would be filled with a weird skewing of chauffeuring, with the white woman driving and the black woman in the back seat as if it were the back of a bus. When I got my license and had to take the maid home, I felt uncomfortable with the seating arrangement, but trying to change it would have been more uncomfortable for both of us.

They always knew much more about us than we did about them. They were chary with details of their personal lives, as if that were all they had to hold onto. We had little idea of what troubled them other than personal sickness or, perhaps, a husband's job loss. Beyond that, they carried their private concerns home to the part of town that most whites never went anywhere near. Seldom did whites see black anger; because of the store we were the exception.

Instead, we whites saw them at their best, their most professional, from the time they let themselves in the back door with their own key until they walked, carrying their paper bags, to the bus stop as the light was failing.

They, however, knew everything about us. They not only witnessed our slovenly habits but cleaned up after them. They observed the most intimate details of our lives, had no choice but to see all our embarrassing personal failings. Details that would never be shared at canasta or at the Women's Club—separate bedrooms, adult tantrums, scattered whiskey bottles—were exposed. Whether it was because of the maids' ubiquity, or because they came from another world, or perhaps because some whites thought them more a utensil than a person, nothing was hidden. So, along with the maids' own unshared lives and their paper bags, they also carried with them all our secrets.

My mother had a succession of maids, some staying with us for years and others for only a few months, but there was never a time while I was growing up that we did not have a maid. While my mother might leave during the day, the maids never did, and they were a constant and comforting presence.

First there was Gladys, who had been my solace in Shreveport; she finally escaped the domestic life when she found a rare office job. I remember Annie Mae, eternally good-natured, who loved to bake and would indulge me in endless games of hide-and-seek. One stern woman, who wouldn't play or even smile, cleaned like a machine. The house was never so spotless or so frightening, and I was happy when a wealthy couple with no children hired her away. Finally there was Melber, at least sixty, diabetic and heavy despite her doctor's warnings, good-humored in the face of desperate family troubles, who stayed with my mother almost until the end.

When I was growing up, our maid arrived in time to clean up after breakfast, and she either caught the last bus home at five-thirty or stayed to clean up after supper and was taken home by my father. Given the primitive state of appliances and household products in the 1950s, a typical day might include waxing or stripping the wax from the linoleum floors, shelling peas, shining silver, defrosting the refrigerator, and ironing endless nonpermanent-press shirts, sheets, and tablecloths. My mother, because of her lack of interest in domestic matters, was not a demanding taskmaster; she was more a sort of on-site absentee landlord. After the basics of cleaning and washing had been accomplished, my mother was not inclined to search out fugitive dust. Sometimes at night she would make up an ambitious list of projects for the maid, and the next day they would go over the list together, but I think they both knew neither would bring it up again. The maid might begin the day with the new projects—scouring baseboards, or cleaning out the junk in the guest room closet, or dusting above the doorways—but soon it was back to hanging clothes out to dry and swiping down the kitchen counters.

In many homes the maids did all the cooking, and white Christian families were happy to sit down to a meal of pork chops, thick biscuits, mashed potatoes with flour gravy, and well-stewed salt-porked vegetables in pot liquor. Southern cooking was basically black cooking, though blacks sometimes used more exotic meats such as chitterlings or pig's feet. My mother would've liked nothing better than to let our maid do the cooking, but her husband and son—especially her son—rebelled, and in truth she didn't like much southern cooking either, though she relished fried chicken and catfish. Every few months she would try again to teach our maid to cook Jewish style, but the graft never took, and soon my mother would be back at the stove.

The maid culture in the South made possible the canasta culture. My mother had her duties—raising me, grocery shopping, keeping the household books, researching the stock market for her weekly tiny investment, and attending temple functions like Hadassah fundraisers. But having a maid all day long created considerable leisure time, which the Jewish ladies filled with canasta, and which their Christian counterparts spent golfing, gardening, and (I am speculating here) attending teas or baby showers where sausage balls were served.

As I grew up, having a maid for five and a half days a week seemed utterly normal, though we weren't wealthy. It was the same in every Jewish household and in the Christian homes I visited. Because I did not see the homes our maids lived in, or the families they left to play hide-and-seek with me, I felt none of the guilt I associated with rent collecting.

In the 1950s, my mother paid Gladys the going rate of twenty dollars per week, a figure that had modestly inflated by Melber's time in 1970 to thirty-five dollars per week, then by 1974 to forty-five dollars. The standard practice throughout the white community was not to pay sick leave. I would like to be able to report that the Jewish community, or at least my mother, applied a more modern and generous approach, but I cannot. According to my mother's ledger for August 23-27, 1971, the usual thirty-five-dollar entry was replaced by twenty-eight dollars with the explanation "1 day ill." Almost harsher is the twenty-one dollars paid for the week of July 14, the lost fourteen dollars in salary explained by "2 days' jury duty."

These draconian entries are balanced by other notations in the faded gray ledger. On August 29, 1973, the ledger indicates, "Loan $500." Melber had, after weeks of hesitation, come to my mother with the story of her son, who had been sitting in the car when his friends robbed a convenience store. He hadn't done anything but had no lawyer, and she had no money. The principal (no interest was charged) was reduced each week by ten dollars from her salary for the next fifty weeks. Melber didn't talk about the case, so my mother didn't ask.

Then, on March 21, 1975, the ledger records a loan of $250. Somehow, Melber's son, a year and a half later, was still sitting in the city jail with no prospect of trial, and she needed another lawyer. My mother suggested Alvin Binder, a local Jewish criminal attorney soon to gain national fame for defending Wayne Williams in the Atlanta child-murder case. We never knew which lawyer Melber hired—she was as private as my mother—but soon thereafter she began to smile again and reported that her son was free. The ten-dollar weekly deductions continued, with the principal occasionally jumping ten, twenty, or thirty dollars for some emergency that threatened to capsize her precarious existence.

Toward the end, when my mother retreated to her books and her "Pearls," Melber's health had deteriorated to the point that she couldn't do much and was more a silent companion than a maid. She could still do light cleaning, and my mother was getting old, too, and what didn't get done didn't get done. They were used to each other after twenty years, the uneducated, gentle, old black woman and the intellectual, sharp-tongued, friendless old Jewish woman. They shared a love of animals; both shamelessly worried and fussed over Herman and Ulysses, the two guinea pigs I'd foisted off on my mother after a failed college romance. They also shared that rarity, a comfortable silence.

When Melber got full Social Security disability and legally couldn't work any more, they awkwardly hugged on her last day, and my mother watched Melber make her way to the corner and step onto the bus for the last time. They talked on the phone every once in a while, especially after my mother got sick, but what could be said when what they had shared was silence and time and just each other's familiar presence? When my father suggested getting another maid, my mother said no, the time for maids was over.

From the time I was born in 1948 until I went off to college, Jackson was utterly segregated. As a child I didn't question the norm that blacks and whites never shared public facilities. The now-startling image, seen in documentaries, of "white" and "colored" drinking fountains was as everyday as a traffic light. It was unremarkable that doctors' offices had a front entrance for whites and a narrow path around back for colored. Nor did I think it odd that LeFleur's, billed as "Jackson's finest restaurant," contained giant murals of plantation life that covered the entire wall. In the painting, minstrel-like slaves smiled as they picked cotton, toted bales onto a riverboat, and served juleps to the master under the shade of the columned big house. Since no black patrons were allowed to eat there, there was never any danger of offending them. As I grew older and less comfortable with the depictions, I observed the all-black bus staff to see their reaction but discerned nothing. For them, the murals were an everyday backdrop to their workday.

It seemed equally natural that there would be separate waiting rooms at the train station near the store, the room for whites spacious with long, gleaming, though uncomfortable, wooden benches, the room for blacks smaller and windowless.

On the train—to Memphis with Gary to visit our cousins, or to New Orleans with my father, supposedly for the Sugar Bowl but really to get a plate of decent spaghetti—the cars were segregated, though in no particular order. As I wandered through the shaking mechanical caravan in search of the rest room, it was always a shock to exit a white car and open the door onto a black one, like stepping into a forbidden world. I—and any black who chanced through a white car—knew instinctively that we possessed only a transit visa and progressed quickly through.

A bigger shock came when I was ten, and my parents took me out of the South, to New York. There, black people acted like white people. They wore suits and ties, they spoke with educated accents, they used the rest room at the hotel, they sat at the next restaurant table. It was disorienting, as if I'd stepped into a racial *Twilight Zone*. When we drove back south, by the time we got into Tennessee the world had shifted back to its familiar shape—the gas stations had white rest rooms and black rest rooms, and blacks spoke as I had heard them speak all my life. Now the familiar seemed oddly off-kilter. Once home, I quickly became reaccustomed to the old social order and comfortably categorized what I'd seen up north as an aberration.

Aware as I was of the differences between myself and the surrounding Christians, I was grateful that we Jews were adjudged to be white. My family and I talked like white people, though perhaps our accents weren't quite so thick. We looked like white people, maybe not as much as I'd have liked, but apparently enough. There were a few specimens of other ethnic groups in Jackson who also didn't look altogether "white"—a handful of Greeks, fewer Italians, even a Mexican, and they were in school with me and thus were deemed white, though with varying success at social acceptance; the Greeks and Italians mixed easily, while the Mexican, it seemed, had barely made it over the line. There were no Asians, so that boggling calculus didn't have to be computed, though I'd heard they went to white schools in the Delta. We weren't Christian, but that wasn't determinative. All that mattered was that we weren't black.

* * *

The Store

In all of Jackson, to my knowledge, Cohen Brothers was the only white-owned business with an integrated rest room and water fountain. The store was small, and there was no room for separate facilities. Had my father and Lazar been so disposed, it would've been in perfect keeping with the times, would not have been bad business or even bad form for a store catering to blacks to have required Will Jones and Marguerite to go to the nearest public black rest room, in our case the train depot a half block away, and to tell customers we had no public rest room. My father and Lazar weren't social radicals, but the equation seemed simple: all-black clientele, all black employees, one rest room. So, on a busy Saturday, there might be a small line outside the store's tiny facility, as Lazar and a customer waited for another customer to finish, while Marguerite peered down from upstairs to ascertain the progress. That small concrete-floored unirace unisex rest room with 1930s-era plumbing and nonfunctioning lock (the room being so cramped that the knees of a person seated on the toilet blocked the door, so there was no need for a lock) was a pre-civil rights era battle site won without a fight or even a protest.

On the issue of race, during the 1950s, my parents and most of the Jewish community were probably more liberal than their counterparts in the Christian community, but only by applying the unexacting standards of the times. We didn't say "nigger," unless by much-regretted accident. We didn't require, or expect, blacks to step aside on the sidewalk. We said hello to blacks on the street. We didn't have separate dishes and silverware for them. When the accused murderer of a black teen, Emmett Till, was let off by an all-white jury, we thought it a terrible injustice, although we said nothing about it except perhaps to each other. We didn't bar the temple door to stop a black from coming to services with a Jewish professor at Tougaloo College, a local black institution. At the store, we called customers "Mr." and "Mrs." when others called men "boy."

All this sounds painfully thin. We observed blacks' humanity, if not their equality, and were sensitive to their feelings. More than that I cannot claim.

In the early 1960s, when I was entering my teens, freedom riders just a bit older than I began coming on buses from northern campuses into Mississippi, a place that for me had always been home, uncomfortable at times but never dangerous. For them, however, it was enemy territory, a battleground. Black voter registration was beginning up in the Delta, and though geographically it was little more than an hour away from my air-conditioned niche in northeast Jackson, I knew nothing about its plantations and poverty. The civil rights organizations, SNCC, COFO, CORE, NAACP, and all the others, were beginning to set up field operations in Mississippi, often in Jackson.

Initially, none of these events affected me. I was in an all-white junior high, and although the Supreme Court had long abolished separate-but-equal schools, it would be still be several years before the first few very token black students filtered into school with me.

The early stirrings of protest first permeated my insulated life on Brook Drive through the daily delivery of the local newspaper, the *Clarion-Ledger*. It was combatively opposed to voter registration and integration, reflecting the view of the vast majority of white Mississippians.

At school, children would parrot their parents' sentiments, and even in the beginning the atmosphere was one of impending invasion and war. In the headlines and in my classmates' tones, there was a sense of outrage and anger and, beneath that, fear.

Most of my schoolmates traced their heritage to before the Civil War. Their oral histories, their deeply imbued family mythologies, told of an invasion from the North exactly a century before. Now their parents feared that blacks, who made up so much of the population and who had been so long suppressed, would one day rise up in anger and overpower them. This dread was sounded in the *Clarion-Ledger*'s stridency and in my schoolmates' braggadocio, and before long would be acted upon.

Fear of a black uprising was not in the southern Jews' well-filled bag of historical phobias. Though some German Jews had been in the South since antebellum days and had fought for the Confederacy, most of us were descended from eastern Europeans who came to the South well after Appomattox, and we simply didn't mine the same vein of history as our white Christian counterparts. Instead, we got our historical boogeymen from grandparents' tales of Cossacks on horseback sweeping through shtetls and of ignorant drunken villagers who thought Jews drank Christian babies' blood at their seders. In the South these villains metamorphosed into their local counterparts, Klansmen and rednecks. Blacks were even more powerless than Jews, and we simply weren't set up psychologically or historically to fear, or hate, them.

As I entered high school in 1963, it was amidst the atmosphere of an all-but-declared civil war. I was not fighting the battles, but the casualties were all around me.

Seale-Lily, an ice cream parlor a mile from my house, served only whites, though it was just across the railroad tracks from a newly black suburban area. I'd sat at its counters since early childhood, but now the round seats had been sawed off, leaving jutting hollow metal poles with sharp edges, gleaming like artillery shells, because blacks had come in to sit down. The lunch counter at Walgreen's on Capitol Street put up a sign: "Closed for Public Safety."

The municipal swimming pool at Riverside Park was another personal Jackson landmark. Set in a shady oak-filled park midway between my house and the store, it was the largest pool in the city, painted with underwater scenes that danced to life under the chlorinated water. To enter the pool we had to run through a maze of showers, trying to avoid the sharp cold spray, emerging soaked and yelling as we jumped into the gigantic pool with all our friends. Of course, all those friends were white.

As soon as black children tried to run through the shower maze, the city simply cut off the water. The pool, along with all other white public pools that hot summer, was drained, and a tall barbed-wire-topped fence strung around it. Separate but equal, the black pools were closed, too, even though there was no threat of integration since no whites would swim in them. The empty Riverside pool looked like a lifeless beached whale, and the paintings of fish on the bottom, without the shimmering water to bring them to life, stared deadly up at the sky. It was surprising to see how fast the cracks appeared, how quickly the weeds sprang up in them. The pool remained closed for years, perhaps a decade, and by the time the social climate had changed enough for the city fathers to consider reopening it, everything was so dilapidated that they just bulldozed dirt into the pool and buried it.

As civil rights leaders began to stage marches downtown, Thompson's Tank was mobilized. Named after the mayor, Allen C. Thompson, the squat ugly armored vehicle came equipped with turrets from which tear gas could be ejected into an unruly crowd. The tank was occasionally taken out for a spin through downtown Jackson as a deterrent; all it did was heighten the sense that a race war was imminent.

Thompson was known as a moderate. In those days, a "moderate" politician was one who, though utterly and vocally in favor of white supremacy, did not openly advocate violence or claim membership in the Klan, which was enjoying a healthy infusion of new blood. In local and state elections, it was these moderate candidates, as opposed to others who called for a virtual armed uprising against the implementation of the 1964 Civil Rights Act, for whom my parents "held their noses" and voted.

Just outside Jackson, Klan rallies were held, advertised by flyers on windshields in white neighborhoods, including mine. One flyer for the "Knights of the Ku Klux Klan" gave a date and time for the rally but no address more specific than "Brandon, Mississippi," adding, "ASK ANY LAW OFFICER FOR DIRECTIONS." Gary and I, foolishly and futilely, spent an entire afternoon removing and disposing of hundreds of them.

The cracks in our world couldn't be patched, were spreading as surely as those in the ruined concrete crater of the Riverside pool. At the store, customers didn't want my father or Lazar to wait on them; they wanted to be waited on by fellow blacks. Will Jones was pressed into service, and Marguerite would be called down even though alterations backed up. Several blacks were hauled off the lunch counter stools at Woolworth's just down the street and beaten. Black children were arrested in the public library a few blocks away, a fact that surprised me, for while I knew and somehow accepted that blacks couldn't swim, eat, or urinate with us, it seemed beyond reason that they couldn't read with us.

On the day of Medgar Evers's funeral, as I walked up Capitol Street from the store, suddenly I found myself in the middle of a surging clash between angry, grieving protesters and shield-bearing riot police. My once-comfortable world was splitting along fault lines between black and white, and like many southern Jews I would find it increasingly difficult to straddle the widening chasm.

During recess at Boyd and in gym at Murrah, the teachers organized a game in which everyone would encircle one person in the middle and try to hit him with a soccer ball. The child in the middle desperately tried to dodge the ball and could only end his torment if by luck he managed to catch it. Then the person who had thrown it would take his turn in the middle. The game was called, by students and teachers alike, "nigger baby." No one remarked on the name. All I could think, as I threw the ball, was that I was glad it wasn't "Jew baby."

I'd worked at cultural anonymity since that first Rosh Hashanah when I was six, just as my predecessors had done when they moved the Sabbath to Sunday. I had been, at different stages in my life, proudly Jewish, then proudly southern, often simultaneously both, and it had always seemed possible to resolve or at least ignore the inherent contradictions. But during the civil rights struggle, my two selves, southern and Jewish, were torn apart.

I was profoundly ambivalent about the coming revolution, as were, I think, most of the Jews in Jackson. One part of me was deeply ashamed of and angry with Mississippi—with the *Clarion-Ledger*'s daily incendiary rhetoric about "mongrelization" and "race mixers," with those surging riot police for that one moment I'd been in their path, with the idiocy of my classmates and their racial slurs, with the mulish intransigence of our leaders. Gary and I, in a gesture as quixotic as stealing the Klan flyers to try to thwart their rally, spat in disgust on the lawn of Ross Barnett's governor's mansion every time we passed, and continued the tradition into the administration of his successor, Paul B. Johnson, Jr. Every new arrest, every new racial murder, made me want to disown my native state, which, along with Alabama, was nationally synonymous with prejudice and hatred.

Yet when I read the pious articles condemning Mississippi in the *New York Times* and the more strident screeds in the *Village Voice*, my southern side would get its back up, with contradictory and equal passion. Self-righteousness had always brought out the rebel in me, and the northerners who'd taken it upon themselves to cure our ills seemed fueled with a healthy dose of it. I knew things were desperately wrong in Mississippi, but, having a southerner's pride, I didn't like being told by outsiders how to fix it. They've got plenty wrong in their own backyards, I thought of the busloads of shining-eyed white students coming down like missionaries.

Today those views sound as politically erroneous as my romantic notions about the Confederacy, but at the time—and now—my state, benighted though it was, was still my state. To those on the outside, to northern Jews, I'm sure Mississippi presented the face of unambiguous evil. Their decision was simple, their opinions unshaded. Their own states' problems needn't be examined in the face of such clear wrong. They didn't have my loyalties, dual and confused though those allegiances were.

One Sunday afternoon near Granny's house, I sat on a hill, along with Gary and Roslyn, watching a group of marchers parade into Jackson, their ranks swelled with Hollywood stars who had come aboard for the last lap. And I, too, felt the sense of invasion I had once scorned in my classmates. Later I felt vindicated when Los Angeles and Detroit and Newark exploded, showing that Mississippi had no monopoly on racial problems.

I was utterly conflicted. I writhed with discomfort yet harbored a secret pride when I saw the disproportionate number of Jewish names in news stories about the white civil rights workers. When I learned that white COFO workers were living with blacks, I remembered those houses, knew I could never live in them—but unbidden came respect, even awe, at the danger these kids not much older than I were exposing themselves to. I had spat on Ross's mansion, but at a local restaurant, when my father introduced me to him, I'd shaken his hand. I detested his politics, but he seemed like a nice man, and at age fifteen I didn't have the courage just to walk away.

In 1965, my senior year in high school, integration finally came to the Jackson public schools. For Murrah this meant that three blacks, outnumbered incalculably more than we Jews, would join the five hundred whites in our class. I remember the first day they came, two girls in Sunday dresses and a thin boy in white shirt and narrow black tie, driven by their parents. The whole student body gathered on either side of the wide front walkway as they came in. Television cameras were there and police, but we were, most of us, from the nice part of town, so there was no taunting, no violence, no movement at all, just the loudest silence. In the halls between classes, no one said anything ugly to them, except once or twice, when one of the rednecks bravely hurled a taunt, like a spitwad. Mostly, no one said anything to them at all.

They tried to stay together, but sometimes the boy's class would be across the building from where the others were, so he would have to wind his way through the silence alone. The two girls seemed to be friends, the smaller, more animated one sometimes smiling at the other, walking together as if in a sealed bubble of ostracism through halls crowded with jostling, flirting, joking white teenagers. The boy seemed set apart even from them, drawing upon some unimaginable inner strength to go it utterly alone, a teenager just my age, who in his old school would've been just a normal kid with friends and sports and girls who might flirt with him. What in God's name had made him volunteer for such a perilous mission, made him willing to go into exile for his cause?

I knew, from my own much less traumatic experience, how difficult being different was, so we had something in common, some little thing. Compared with the other 1499 Murrah students, there were probably fewer degrees of separation between us. Very probably his parents traded at the store, perhaps regularly, were known to my father by name, had shopped there for clothes for their son to wear as he went off to the equivalent of war.

As I had with Marguerite's sons, I thought about approaching the boy as he walked quickly between classes, to say hello, just to show that all white people weren't prejudiced. I practiced my speech but never gave it. At graduation, because of alphabetical happenstance, he sat right beside me, walked behind me to receive our diplomas. At rehearsal, when the seating became known, other boys would razz me: "Cohen's got to sit by the nigger." I didn't smile, but I didn't correct them either.

As the atmosphere everywhere in the city became more and more inflamed, Jackson's Jews felt the increased polarization. At the store a tense truce prevailed, but the old easy ambience, the temporary camaraderie of commerce, was replaced by curtness. When Will Jones's son married, a large reception was held at Collins Funeral Home, and, despite the growing divide, my father and mother and Lazar and Lolita attended. Will Jones's long-time Jewish doctor, Max Berman, spent several uncomfortable minutes with a black patient, her anger freed by the times and the social surroundings, as she at last expressed her outrage at the indignity of the universal southern custom of segregated waiting rooms. Though Max sympathized, even agreed with her, he also knew that his many white patients wouldn't tolerate a black person in the same waiting room. As always, we had to try to balance everything carefully to see which way we would lose less.

Our equilibrium was unstable, our strategies convoluted. Another Jewish doctor whose office was on "Pill Hill" near Memorial Stadium, where Ole Miss football games were played, was chided by a fellow Jew about his "colored entrance." The doctor should let his black patients enter through the front, the friend said, and he suggested a plan for accomplishing this controversial innovation. In order not to be seen removing the sign himself, the doctor should wait until the night of a football game, then under cover of darkness remove the sign, blame it on the rowdy football crowd and quietly integrate his waiting room, without taking a stand.

Rabbi Perry Nussbaum was one Jew who did not equivocate about civil rights. From the first Friday night that he stood behind the pulpit, the congregation knew his tenure was not going to be a comfortable one. His abrasive personality was coupled with an integrity about principles that simply left no room for the niceties of public opinion, either of his own congregation or of the conservative Christian community he found himself in. Nor, apparently, in his makeup was there any room for fear.

In the early days of his tenure, even before the first tremors of change were felt, Rabbi Nussbaum often used his sermon to chastise us about our complacency. When the protests began, when the "outside agitators" started to arrive, when Medgar Evers set up his NAACP field office in Jackson not far from the store, the rabbi's sermons became more pointed, contending that we Jews had been slaves, that Mississippi was a modern-day Egypt and that, no matter how few we were, it was our duty to march on the side of right.

The rabbi's outspoken support of civil rights illuminated the split between southerner and Jew in the congregation. Some few in the temple were liberals and even, it was reputed, had blacks as social guests in their homes. Some few others were openly racist in their views and might have found the Klan compatible except for the inconvenient fact of their Jewishness. Most of us, though, hovered uncomfortably in the middle, trying to reconcile the ethical absolutes of Judaism with the equally absolute norms of our Christian neighbors. We might've been strangers in the land of Egypt, but we were in many ways strangers in the South, too, welcomed but very aware that our welcome could easily be revoked.

Rabbi Nussbaum was not concerned with southern hospitality. Nor was his advocacy of civil rights limited to our cloistered Jewish world. He was prominently—too prominently, many would say—involved in numerous ecumenical marches. I listened to his sermons and read about his marches with the same feelings of tortured ambivalence I had toward the entire civil rights movement. My aversion to his insistent, abrasive *hoching* (nagging) was equalled, sometimes even surpassed, by my admiration for his courage.

The store, and, by extension, Capitol Street, had always been familiar and friendly territory to me. To the NAACP and many blacks, Capitol Street was occupied by the enemy—anything but friendly—and I saw, despite the daily intertwining of my family's lives with black people's, that an almost unbridgeable chasm of incomprehension lay between us.

In spring 1963, the Jackson NAACP imposed a boycott on all white-owned Capitol Street merchants, including Cohen Brothers. The major goals were the use of courtesy titles ("Mr." and "Mrs.") for black customers, the hiring of black employees, and the elimination of segregated water fountains and rest rooms in stores.

Though Cohen Brothers had long since voluntarily satisfied these demands, other white storeowners found them radical. For them, to call a black "Mr." was unthinkable. One large store with substantial black trade had two water fountains, one unabashedly marked "white only." According to a May 29, 1963, *Clarion-Ledger* article, the NAACP urged Jackson Mayor Allen Thompson to "press local businessmen to open their dining and rest room facilities on an equal basis." The mayor's reply: "Such things are up to the businessmen."

The boycott began to cut deeply into Cohen Brothers' business. When my father and Lazar asked the NAACP for an exemption from the boycott, they were told to put pressure on the white establishment. Unlikely and powerless emissaries though they were, they tried.

They did not succeed. Stores with mostly white clientele remained unaffected by the boycott, and larger stores with mixed trade could still depend on their white business. These stores had war chests of capital reserves to withstand the onslaught, and some had branches in suburban shopping centers—which were only nominally included in the boycott. Black customers who normally shopped at a Capitol Street store simply patronized its branch. Cohen Brothers had no white trade, no war chest, and no branches.

Thousands of boycott posters were distributed in the black community, reading, "Negro Shoppers! Don't buy on Capitol Street," and watchers for the boycott were placed in front of the larger stores like Woolworth's to dissuade black shoppers from entering.

Lazar printed a sign on the primitive store press—"We deliver"—hoping it might attract customers afraid of going against the boycott. My father and Lazar were moving backward into peddling as they loaded socks, underwear, or a shirt through the back door and drove it to the few customers willing to risk shopping with us.

My father and Lazar went back to the white businessmen, continuing their fruitless shuttle diplomacy, but the NAACP's demands were viewed by the establishment as an abomination, an attack on a way of life, and not to be borne.

Capitol Street became the major battle zone of Jackson's civil rights war. According to Medgar Evers's widow in her book, *For Us, the Living*, it was "the street that symbolized our frustrations." The boycott was only part of it. Massive protest marches were held, followed by equally massive arrests, with protesters jailed in livestock barns on the state fairgrounds down the hill from the Old Capitol. We could see it all just by standing in front of the store, bystanders caught in history.

In the newspapers, on television, at the temple, there was realistic talk of a race war. At home, my father said "nigger" and we battled over it, one of the few times anger was set free in our household.

"The same people who say 'nigger' are the ones who're going to say 'kike,' " I said heatedly.

He didn't have an answer to that. I don't think he even looked for one, so charged had become the situation downtown, where he was daily and unwillingly on the front lines.

"If it comes down to a war, I know which side I'll be on." And for that one moment he meant it.

The store slowly starved. In May 1963, the sales for the entire month didn't equal one day's receipts prior to the boycott. Day after day passed without a single customer coming into the store. My father drove out to the shopping centers; they were thriving. The boycott might continue forever, and, even if it ended, their customers might never come back. The store had been in operation for over sixty years, but now it faced extinction. Despite our compliance, the rabbi and the liberals in the congregation sided with the boycott, against us. For them, ideology outweighed the ties of what I, in my childhood, had thought of as an extended Jewish family.

All along, my father and Lazar had been pleading with the NAACP. Now an extraordinary session was convened at Cohen Brothers, with the NAACP representatives sitting in the shoe department. Our hopes were raised because the session seemed more formal. Uncle Melvin—the old Boston lawyer—pleaded Cohen Brothers' case. All around the store, the empty shelves from cancelled orders, the utter absence of customers, showed how effective the boycott had been. They listened quietly. At the end, they stood and left, as uncompromising as the white establishment. Both were fighting for a way of life, one old, one new, and if there were civilian casualties, such were the costs of war.

After two years, the boycott quietly dissipated. Customers slowly started shopping at Cohen Brothers again, but not the old customers, who were uncomfortable reappearing after so long an absence. Very gradually relationships began to form between the Cohens and their new black customers, but it wasn't the same. Leonard and Lazar were getting older, the civil rights battle continued to rage on other fronts for several more years, and downtown never quite came back.

Even after the boycott, I wanted to make the store my profession—it was a family tradition, the sole remaining Cohen institution. But, to his credit, my father discouraged me. Perhaps he'd seen me writing at the store, or perhaps he wanted to show me the reality of what I'd often heard him say, that it was "no way to live, walking the same thousand square feet every day of your life."

I was persistent. So he did something very difficult for him: he cracked down on me. The only precedent had been when I was ten and lost two dollars in the slot machines at the Colonial Country Club. I had turned to my father, the softhearted parent, the one who'd always make it right, and was stunned when he said I'd lost the money and now it was gone. The gambler was teaching me an elementary lesson in consequences.

His cure for my store career was equally simple. He suggested, when I came home from college my sophomore summer, that I work at the store to "see how you like it." Business was good again, the boycott receding into memory. The difference between that summer and all my previous Saturdays and Christmas Eves was that I was treated as an employee, not as a son. That meant no visiting with old friends when they came to hang out at the store as they had for years. No coming in at ten o'clock and leaving at four; I worked from nine until six every weekday and until six-thirty on Saturday. No swimming at the Patio Club pool up at the King Edward even when Ralph came in to announce that lots of girls were there. And no writing and no reading. It took only a month to remedy my enthusiasm for carrying on the family tradition.

My father knew the store was dying. Before, he had walked up Capitol Street and seen the business going to other stores. Now he saw no business anywhere on the street; everyone was at the new Jackson Mall or at Westland Plaza shopping center. Cohen Brothers had crested, with respect to location, back in Moise and Sam's time, when the train station was the town center. The store had survived in the backwater as the business wave moved farther up the street. Now the store was a virtual island.

All around, through the 1970s and into the early 1980s, businesses were closing, either moving to the shopping centers or giving up. Across the street, the King Edward Hotel locked its doors and half the block went dark. Soon, in an area that had once housed over fifteen retail establishments, the store's only neighbors were the poolroom that, cockroach-like, couldn't be killed, and a newly opened pornographic bookstore.

They kept working, though they were getting well into their seventies, my father, Lazar, Marguerite, Will Jones. My father was thinner, weaker, not quite believing he wasn't the Tiger of Tulane. Lazar, still with an enviably thick head of hair, now white, had leg problems that made rising from his chair a test of will. By this time in their lives, Moise and Sam had been receiving well wishers in the shoe department, but Gary and I weren't on the bench to relieve the tired old guard. Marguerite, always frail, moved her fingers more slowly on the ancient machine she had always favored. Will

Jones, the red in his hair surviving only in his nickname, couldn't do much except stand at the front and greet customers.

The neighborhood was getting bad. Burglars sawed their way in through the roof of the long-shuttered Capitol Hotel, or smashed through the glass front door, or lowered themselves from the skylight. The security service would call my father at four in the morning, just as renters had once done, but now he was seventy-five. He would pick up Lazar, seventy-seven, to drive down in time to greet the dawn and the just-arriving police.

Word got out on the street that the store was a ghost ship manned by a helpless geriatric crew, and shoplifters appeared like rats. They would brazenly grab ties and shirts and belts and walk out, not particularly fast. One man ventured far into the store, grabbed an armful of suits, and started out, hugging them to his chest. Forgetting he wasn't a half century younger, my father tried to grab the suits, but the man twisted them away. My father's finger was cut by the metal hanger, and his glasses fell to the floor, but he gave chase down Capitol Street until the thief outpaced him, still gripping his prize. I couldn't help admiring the sheer age-defying foolhardiness of it, but my mother was less appreciative. (My father had recently, over her protest, insisted on cleaning pine straw from the gutters on the roof of the house and had accidentally kicked the ladder out from under himself, which left the septuagenarian hanging by his fingertips from the gutter.)

My mother became increasingly worried about his safety and, as her concern mounted, so did her irritation at his insistence on keeping the store open. While he was driving to Hinds General Hospital (to get a tetanus shot for the cut from the metal hanger), she called to enlist me in her campaign. My father thought perhaps he could squeeze a few more years out of the store, maybe ten. They hadn't let the boycott kill them; why should mere mortality? But my mother looked at the store and at my father without illusion. She remembered her father and the Seven-Up bottle. I called my father that night. It was odd to be on my mother's side against him, but, like her, I'd seen what he was unwilling to see.

"It's not safe any more," I told him. "Word's gotten out you're an easy target and you've just been lucky so far they haven't come in with a gun to rob you."

"We don't keep that much cash in the store," he evaded, trained by Etta. There wasn't much fight in his voice, and that made me sad. But the job had to be finished.

"You're two old men and you could get killed. It's time to retire. Time to close the store."

After a long pause, he said, "I know."

Even so, they delayed the inevitable. As long as one cap remained to be sold, there was a reason to keep the store open. For protection (from my mother as well as thieves) they hired a security service, "for presence," as the detective agency described it, but the presence was dispiriting for shoppers and Cohens alike. The young security guards would glare suspiciously at all customers, and the older ones caught shoplifters only in their dreams.

In 1988, the year of the store's ninetieth anniversary, Cohen Brothers was the oldest retail establishment in Jackson, run by the city's oldest merchants. Lazar was seventy-eight, my father seventy-six. Will Jones had finally been ordered by his doctor to stay at home. Marguerite could only make it in a couple of days a week.

Finally, they held the unimaginable, a going-out-of-business sale. Ellis Hart, a retired Jewish friend who himself had operated a *shtorke*, relished the chance to get back into the trade, and the three old men, cutting the deals of a lifetime, managed to move almost all the stock. On the very final day, my wife, Kathy, and I drove down to Capitol Street with a bottle of Scotch, as I had done on all those Christmas Eves past. The store looked bereft, barren of merchandise, and my father and Lazar looked both relieved and utterly lost. Outside, we took a photo of my father shaking the door twice, to be sure it was locked, then going back to shake it one very last time.

After the closing, it was amazing how soon the life went out of the place. They kept the electricity going for a while, like a respirator on a patient the family won't let go. Then that went, too, and, as the old tin roof started to leak, the store became a building, then a musty-smelling shell as the Big House had been after the old folks left. Always the archivist, I wanted to salvage what I could. My father let me in. The long narrow room seemed much smaller without all the customers. Many of the display cases had been sold, and the space looked much as it had when Moise and Sam first built it.

I wanted to take it all, to save it all. If I could have, I would have moved the whole store to my backyard. I had only a friend's borrowed truck, but I managed to take away the table where Uncle Ike had spread his swatches when he told Moise about Etta, the gift-wrap table where Pearle, Lolita, Roslyn, Marguerite, and my mother had an assembly line on Christmas Eve day, and finally the old cash register, weighing no less than six hundred pounds, the "A" and "B" buttons obliterated from the millions of finger marks left by every Cohen I'd ever known.

The Lost Tribe

"I didn't think Jews lived in Mississippi. I didn't think *anybody* lived there."
University of Miami student

"What part of the island are you from?"
Another Miami student, referring to Long Island in a question to me

In 1966, my senior year at Murrah, I began to implement my old escape plan. Everything at Murrah and outside it concentrated my focus. Not only was I hunted in the halls by a boy the size of a tree stump whose dim fancy had fixed on a girl I was dating, but one of the coaches caught me not dressing out, and I had to wear the white "Jackson Public Schools" shorts and participate in organized sports. And even though the '60s rebellion hadn't yet come to Mississippi, I was continuing to absorb the sedition of my *Village Voice* and letting my hair grow, its progress closely monitored by the crew-cut coaches. In the larger world, as the civil rights struggle continued to intensify, almost every night on the news I saw Mississippi cast as the national villain, and every morning I read the *Clarion-Ledger*'s maddening response.

I applied to Tulane (though New Orleans really wasn't far enough away for me) and to North Carolina and Duke and even to some junior colleges in exotic California. I didn't know where I wanted to go, just what I wanted to get away from.

Virtually everyone else at Murrah, including all my friends, would be staying in state. I'd known Jimmy Crell since Boyd days, and Cliff Camp since junior high, and had weathered innumerable campouts with them in Mississippi's mosquito-infested woods, including one near-mythic experience when, soon after Will Jones dropped us off, Noah-proportion rains washed out our frail campsite, and we wandered lost most of the moonless night, subsisting on sodden marshmallows. I had almost never been without them as constant friends.

Ole Miss, the University of Mississippi, claimed the majority of my classmates, who would encounter four more years of Murrah—the unrelenting caste system, the religion of football, the cult of clothes, and the worship of beauty— but with all of the competition formalized by fraternities and sororities. Future wives would meet future lawyer and doctor husbands who would meet future clients and patients. Mississippi State, Crell and Camp's destination, drew future engineers, pre-vet students, and nonmembers of the social elite (some by choice), who would've withered at Ole Miss. Mississippi Southern, where Ralph would go, had the uncontested reputation as the easiest and least traditional state school. I was terrified of going to a college where I knew no one, but I never even momentarily considered any of them.

Though a state school would have been much less expensive, my parents didn't contest my decision. Few Jackson Jews ever went to state schools. Lazar had gone off to Syracuse before the cold drove him back south to Tulane, where his transcript garbled his first name to "Tarzan," forever after his nickname. Though never a scholar, my father also went to Tulane, and when his grades fell, he transferred not to a Mississippi school but to the University of Alabama to rehabilitate his GPA so he could return. Pearle, even less academically inclined than my father, whiled away a few semesters at L.S.U. In my generation, Janice was already at the University of Texas, Buddy's daughter Marilyn had been accepted at L.S.U., and Roslyn was scrambling as feverishly as I to get across the state line.

The obstacle to my escape was my grades. As my mother noted daily, I was not realizing my potential. My rebellion against everything, which had started when I left Boyd, extended to my studies, and I had calculated and exerted the precise effort necessary to achieve a C in every subject. My standing hovered unimpressively around the middle of the

166

class. Still, my verbal SAT score was high, and I hoped that would compensate. As for math, my brain seemed to lack the necessary cortex. My mother had spent endless hours dutifully, if not patiently, going over and over train problems, teaching what to her seemed perfectly simple concepts, while I desperately but unsuccessfully tried to grasp them just to spare myself her sharp, "Edward Charles, how many times do I have to explain that?" I thrashed at chemistry for a couple of weeks, like a tired swimmer who knows he's going to drown, then gave up and received not an F but an unprecedented zero.

Everyone had been accepted somewhere by the time my first rejection, from Duke, arrived. Vanderbilt and Columbia came the next week, in the same batch of mail, and North Carolina followed soon after. Tulane, which had benched my father, wouldn't even let me try out. I was glad I'd had the forethought to apply, over my mother's objection, to those obscure California junior colleges with their brochures of beachside volleyball tourneys. Then, one by one, they rejected me.

As I considered Ole Miss, State, and Southern, like three very different but equally effective suicide plans, I received something novel—an acceptance letter—from the University of Miami, to which I had randomly applied and then forgotten about. I remembered Miami had nice beaches and hotels. About the school I knew nothing except that it met my two criteria: it wasn't in Mississippi and it would let me in.

As the day approached for my departure for Miami, I began to realize the enormity of what I had undertaken. Everyone I knew was going to schools no more than three hours' drive away. Many planned to go home on weekends, and, should an emergency, real or imaginary, arise, home was a straight shot down the highway. Miami was a full two-day drive, at the bottom of an endless peninsula. Despite all my bluster and bravado about leaving Mississippi and never returning, I listened with envy as Camp and Crell made plans to room with each other at State. They'd have each other, while I would be living in a gigantic city where I knew no one. Classmates much more secure and confident than I weren't venturing out of state. Who did I think I was? I got out the giant atlas my mother kept in the den beneath *The World's Great Religions* and saw that the cartographic nit that represented Jackson would fit ten times into the engulfing coastal lesion that marked Greater Miami.

I made the few preparations I could. Because of the store and my father's indulgence, my wardrobe was as vast as my insecurity. I had ten pairs of shoes, button-down shirts of every stripe and check, socks to match every shirt, as many pants as I had shirts, wool suits in case of a climatic shift, and four alligator belts (black, brown, navy blue, and olive green).

Since the days of the almost-rabid dog bite, and long before, my father had taken care of all contingencies, imaginable and otherwise. He had always filled all the family cars with gas in the early morning hours, so that the actual process of filling a gas tank remained as mysterious to me as nuclear fission. If I had an appointment, he'd often drive there the night before to scout out the route in order to warn me of tricky turns; now how would I find anything? If I needed money, the bank of Cohen had always been open, but now I struggled to absorb my mother's crisp instructions on how to write a check on my new Deposit Guaranty Bank checking account. I wondered what kind of people went to the University of Miami and whether there would be any Jews there.

Although information about the school was sparse in Mississippi, I had deduced that if I didn't get into a fraternity, I would be an outsider for the next four years, never meeting a girl or making a friend. I had hoped that by eluding the Murrah/Ole Miss caste system I might somehow prosper socially, but a fraternity was by definition a group, and I'd never done well in groups, had in fact rebelled against them. I began to worry that I wouldn't get what I didn't want. My father and Lazar, who at Tulane had both been in a Jewish fraternity, ZBT, wrote the Miami chapter, speaking of my "solid citizenship" and "enthusiastic spirit."

"You'll make contacts you'll use all your life in business," my father told me. He still saw me as ultimately engaging in some kind of normal profession like insurance, and now not only the next four years but the entire rest of my life apparently was at stake.

One by one, my friends left Jackson, driven by their parents to the nearby college towns of Oxford, Starkville, Hattiesburg. As for me, the college I in my wisdom had chosen required an airplane flight to get to, like Tibet.

My mother had excelled at the University of Illinois, with a Latin major. My father after two years had dropped out of Tulane because, as he put it, "I was just wasting my father's money." As my parents and I boarded the plane for Miami, the unasked question was, in whose footsteps would I follow?

At the Eden Roc Hotel (known to regulars as the "Yidden Roc") in Miami Beach, we checked in for a short vacation before registration day. I studied for the hundredth time the glossy literature the school had sent, trying to divine from the photographs of tanned, smiling, purposeful-looking students whether my escape plan had been horribly ill conceived. The brochure depicted an air-conditioned high-rise dorm, where, according to official correspondence, I would not be living. I was assigned to one of several unair-conditioned apartments for four, not illustrated.

So was Eric, a fellow freshman I met while walking on the hotel beach. Eric was unlike anything Mississippi had prepared me for, a surfer from New Jersey, with an enviable swoop of sunbleached hair that sailed along his face just above his eyes. He knew almost as little about the school as I but wasn't worried because Miami had great year-round surf. He was equally unconcerned, having never encountered a southern summer, that he hadn't gotten into the air-conditioned dorm.

"Which apartment are you in?" he asked.

"30-E," I said. I had puzzled over the number all summer, trying unsuccessfully to divine size, number of floors, and luxuriousness from the numeral and letter.

He looked amazed. "I am, too."

The statistical improbability of two roommates chancing to meet and identify each other in a megalopolis of one million did not seal our friendship—we recognized how different we were—but it was enough for Eric to propose an adventure to a Miami Beach nightclub he'd heard about.

I had been to nightclubs before in Las Vegas, but always with my parents. I'd never conceived of going to one by myself. The unremarkable fact that Miami was a very large city struck me with renewed force.

Eric seemed much more worldly than I, and I had the first intimation of the feeling I would struggle with for the rest of my time in Miami: that I was a rustic, a rube, a bumpkin. Everybody in Mississippi was, only they'd had the good sense not to have to realize it. My friends at Ole Miss and Mississippi State weren't having to worry about going to nightclubs; in their sane world they were getting their heads shaved by upperclassmen so that freshman girls wouldn't go out with them. Hadn't I wanted to escape Mississippi and everyone and everything in it? Hadn't the *Village Voice* prepared me for a voyage into the vast world waiting just outside the Magnolia State? As we roared through the still-busy nighttime urban streets on Eric's motorcycle, I could've been safe in my bed at the Edec Roc, even safer tucked in on Brook Drive.

Instead we were pulling into a very cosmopolitan-looking club. Inside, sophisticated women of twenty, wearing imported-looking high-heeled sandals, were dancing with urbane men of twenty-two, dressed in white shoes that flashed in the murky room like semaphore flags signalling that I was a h-i-c-k.

"You guys go to the university?" asked a voice in the darkness. I recognized the accent as undiluted New York, vowels twisting beyond normal inclinations, consonants stepping on each with casual assurance.

Two boys our own age were sitting at the next table. Both were from Great Neck, Long Island. If coolness and savvy could be depicted, as on one of those charts that show how recent a development civilization is, Jackson would be somewhere at ape level, Eric's home on the New Jersey shore would be early Neanderthal, and Great Neck would be too evolved to fit on the graph.

Danny was Italian and wore wire-rim glasses, like beatniks I'd seen pictured in the *Village Voice*. His friend, Peter, was Jewish, with dark furtive eyes, and he spoke in a sort of hepcat musician's argot.

With them was a girl, a northern Jewish girl, the first I'd encountered. I was amazed that a girl other than a relative could be named Cohen. I found myself dancing with her. It felt like a cross between incest and lunar exploration without a space suit. She was doing some sort of advanced dance movement that would reach Mississippi in about twenty years. I shuffled about, bobbing arrhythmically as if trying to dislodge a turnip caught in my throat—my exclusion from the seventh-grade rock 'n' roll class had had crippling repercussions. I didn't speak to her. By saying nothing, I avoided revealing how little I knew about everything that I knew she knew everything about.

The Lost Tribe

Back at the table, Eric—who now, by comparison, seemed as normal and familiar as my parents—was talking with Danny and Peter. He asked them their room assignments.

"30-E," said Danny.

"30-E," said Peter.

Somehow the four occupants of the same campus apartment had managed to converge in the vastness of Miami. Whatever amazement I had at the improbability or significance of this confluence was secondary to the fact that the nameless faceless alien world I had feared now had names and faces, and they were far more exotic than anything I could have imagined from my eighteen years in the pine-speckled suburbs of Mississippi.

The drive with my parents from Miami Beach to Coral Gables took only thirty minutes, but it was filled with last-minute exhortations, encouragements, and worries.

"You'll make friends," my mother assured me.

"Don't let anybody take advantage of you or push you around." My father looked around at me in the back. We were off the expressway and onto surface streets, a sign of impending arrival.

"Don't be too trusting," he continued. "If you have any problems, go to the dean. Or call me. I could fly down."

"That won't be necessary," my mother's voice sharpened.

"Have you got enough cash?"

We turned onto the campus and I felt its hugeness reach into the car and wash over me. The university was nothing like the sleepy Mississippi colleges I'd seen. There wasn't any shade, only endless pylons of palms that made me think I was not in another state but another hemisphere. Plants that in Mississippi I'd seen confined to small pots here grew outside to outlandish sizes. My parents no longer could protect me; this was bigger than they. They were now merely powerless escorts.

My father turned at a sign that read "Apartments 26-34." We passed small, squat two-story concrete bunker-like buildings. The freshman apartments had previously been married students' dorms, before the married students had refused to live in them. In their parking lots other parents were letting off their children. No one looked happy. We pulled into the parking lot of Building 30. My mother looked at my new home.

"Maybe next year you can get into the dorm" was her only comment.

"Sure he can. Next year he can get into the dorm," my father echoed, heartily if hollowly.

Inside, it was spartan. Eric's belongings were neatly unpacked. He apparently was already out fearlessly exploring the campus. His wardrobe in the closet consisted of a few T-shirts and an alternate pair of flip-flops.

It was as hot as the day of Uncle Sig's seder, and I knew that in Miami summer never ended. My father and I set up the electric fan so it would blow on me as I slept. My mother made my bed, and I realized suddenly there would be no maid to change the sheets next week. How would they get changed, or for that matter, washed? Who would do it?

Finally nothing was left to unpack or rearrange, and the moment arrived for them to leave. I had not anticipated how bereft I would feel. I was an only child whose parents had been unusually attentive, all the more so because they, too, had grown up as Jews in the South and knew the importance of insulation from the surrounding world.

My father cried, and I cried. My mother, whose tears I had seen only a very few times, hugged me, and I could feel her jagged breath catching before she brought it under control. Desperate to delay the ultimate moment, my father suggested that they drive down that night to eat supper with me, but my mother shook her head: it was time. I watched their car pull out of the parking lot. I think my mother must have driven because my father had never stopped crying. They would stay the night at the hotel before flying back home, but it already seemed as though they were irretrievably gone.

The morning of registration, determined not to look like a hick, I dressed carefully—Murrah High School button-down shirt, cuffed Cohen Brothers pants, shined wing tips. Everyone else wore shorts and shower flip-flops like Eric's. As far as I could see were people I didn't know, and, despite Miami's southernmost location, a large percentage of them appeared to be from the North and to be Jewish.

Miami Beach was on the vacation migratory route from New York to Miami, a direct flight, one Jew following another, just as my ancestors had found their way to Mississippi. New Yorkers escaping winter could count on finding their neighbors in the gigantic hotel lobbies or playing gin in cabanas. Their children had followed. So had I, but the route, both geographically (through Atlanta, with a three-hour layover) and emotionally was much more complicated.

While my Murrah classmates banded together, shaven-headed, in their strange new environments, I shuffled alone from class to class. Despite the cosmic coincidence of our first meeting, I saw little of my roommates. We were just too different, or at least I felt we were, and as always that was enough to distance me from them. I put my wing tips (sweet potato tan) in the back of my closet and switched to penny loafers, which more closely resembled shower thongs.

Remembering the warnings, I signed up for fraternity rush. My parents had assumed I would pledge a Jewish fraternity, just as they later assumed I would marry a Jewish girl, but, having spent my life surrounded by Christians, I saw no reason to rule out their fraternities. I soon learned, however, that the Christian houses did not accept Jews. Even so, we still had to go through the charade of visiting every Christian fraternity—Sigma Chi, SAE, Lambda Chi, and all the others—pilgrimaging on foot with bright smiles to closed shrines.

Nothing in Mississippi—my High Holyday inquisition, my exclusion from the rock 'n' roll class, the boys who called each other "Hebrew" and "Rabbi"—had made me feel as conspicuously Jewish as did those smiling blond brothers, with their quick appraisal of my genetic probabilities, a practiced glance at my name tag confirming the suspicion, and then an arm placed around the next boy in line whose name tag and forebears passed initial muster. We had to stay at each house for thirty minutes, but it didn't take ten before the Jews in our group huddled together near the exit like rejected livestock.

When we came to the four Jewish houses, the rejected spavined cattle suddenly became blue-ribbon breeding stock. Brothers put their arms on my shoulders. Southernness wasn't an impediment, my Jewishness being far more important. Suddenly, without having done anything except being born, I seemed to possess the secret key to the club. I was an M.O.T.: a member of the tribe.

ZBT was the largest, most prestigious Jewish fraternity, I learned from the ZBT brothers. These were not rustic Jackson Jews. Many were from New York, and others were from Shaker Heights, Ohio, the richest community in the country. One brother was the scion of a mighty peanut butter family. Another wore an ascot. I was at the edge of the great wide world I'd always yearned for.

Although the bid process was supposed to be inviolately secret, during the next week of waiting I approached some of the brothers who seemed to like me. When all I got was cryptic smiles, I worried that I shouldn't have spoken to them, that perhaps I'd turned a friend into a blackball.

I called home. The ill-hidden worry in my father's voice undercut my flimsy self-assurances, and I derived even less comfort from my mother's fatalistic "If you don't get in, you'll survive." I knew better; I knew that it would be rock 'n' roll class all over again, except that this time I would have been cast out by my own.

The pledge class of 1966 gathered in a large hall to receive sealed envelopes containing either bids or . . . nothing, except a mimeographed form from the Interfraternity Council saying that there were many campus organizations, such as the School Spirit Club, for independents to join.

The line progressed very slowly. Some rushees, unable to wait, blocked the line while they opened their envelopes. I saw several people yell in excitement, and as many walk out silently, next stop the School Spirit Club. Finally I was handed my envelope. It seemed very light, precisely the weight of a #10 envelope and a strip of mimeographed paper. Somehow I stepped to the side, tore open the envelope (receiving a paper cut), and thrust my bleeding hand inside. Nothing! No, one thing. A pledge card from—ZBT!

At the fraternity house, I was warmly welcomed. A life of belonging was at last beginning.

Alone among campus fraternities, the ZBT brothers, emulating the Ivy League schools they hadn't gotten into, required all pledges to wear ties—identical maroon-and-navy striped ties. At first I didn't mind. Then, particularly on days when I wore clashing brown or green pants, I began to feel a tiny constriction, an infinitesimal rebellion. I ignored it; I had found my tribe.

It was made up of Jews very different from me, Jews plugged into the main line of Jewish culture and identity, Jews who had no cultural dichotomy. My pledge class was filled with fast-talking boys from Long Island who seemed to know the score on everything from horseracing to the phone numbers of the best-looking Jewish girls to what to order at Wolfie's Delicatessen. I, however, didn't know in which direction to cut a bagel in half. There were a few southern Jews in the fraternity—soft-spoken courteous boys from Memphis and Atlanta and New Orleans—but for my friends I wanted the real thing. I knew what I wanted to be when I grew up—a New York Jew.

The landmarks and memories that these Jews shared were as alien to me as the altar of Jackson's First Baptist Church. Everyone else was from The City or one of a hundred hamlets on Long Island where they all had a history and a place in some larger northern society that had transported itself down to Miami. Similarly, my friends from Murrah who had gone to State and Southern and Ole Miss had transferred their class status, for good or ill, with them. It was a starting point, even if much diluted by all the new blood from a hundred other high schools. Most freshmen had fixed references in the enemies and friends they'd known for twelve solid years. They might've wished to be anonymous, pastless, like me, but they had chosen the familiar evil. And I'd chosen the unfamiliar. I was a lost tribe of one. Everyone else knew holidays like Simchas Torah, and I knew Confederate Memorial Day.

When, years before as a child, I had stretched my concept of reality to encompass the gigantic southern Christian universe, it was as much of an accommodation as I thought I could ever make. Now my view was again expanding, this time to take in an equally enormous northern Jewish world, and it was no less unsettling than the first time.

I had thought that being Jewish would be all the link I needed, but to these purebred northern Jews I was an exotic half-breed, an object of curiosity, amusement, and scorn. The South was unthinkable, a bumpkin patch.

"I didn't think *anyone* lived there," they said, and they meant it. It beggared their imagination to conceive that human beings, except for redneck sheriffs and their victims, really occupied that obscure vertical wedge of land somewhere down on the far end of the map.

"Do *Jews* live there?"

My mere existence was utterly unsettling to their borough-centric view of the universe. My fellow pledges, from Newark and Brooklyn and Philly, knew about my home only from the movies and the news. The movies about Mississippi, such as *In the Heat of the Night*, were portraits of unrelieved backwardness and bigotry. In the news, unfortunately, the truth regarding Mississippi more than matched the fiction. The murder of the three civil rights workers in Philadelphia, Mississippi, was very recent when I arrived at Miami, as was the slaying of Medgar Evers in Jackson.

In 1967, I had just returned to school for my sophomore year when my parents called to tell me the Ku Klux Klan had bombed the new Jackson temple, which had been consecrated only a few months before. Rabbi Nussbaum had been one of very few white clergymen in Mississippi to speak out for civil rights, though his activism caused bitter dissension among the congregants. For most, fitting in meant being segregationist or keeping safely quiet if you weren't. On Brook Drive we were in the latter—the safe—camp.

Two months later, the Klan bombed the rabbi's house. My cousin Gary, not yet in college, felt the floors of his bedroom shake from the explosion three miles away. Miraculously, Rabbi Nussbaum and his wife, who were home at the time of the blast, were uninjured.

In Miami, as the bombings and other horrors flashed across the nightly news and into the *Miami Herald* headlines, I found myself on trial. I was a Mississippian, the only one my fellow students had ever seen or were likely to see. I learned I had another secret self—and that self was southern. I grew to dread that point in a conversation when we all told where we were from. I wished I could say something normal, like "Queens" or "Hewlett" or "Jersey" or even "Shaker Heights." It wasn't only that, once I'd admitted my origin, I became the proxy for all their anger and derision. It was that I was again alien, and, to someone who always had been, that was unsupportable. I'd gotten to the Promised Land, but I didn't meet the residency requirement.

The question of my identity would be my most demanding course of instruction in college. I was as determined as I had been in Mississippi not to be different. To join the tribe, I annihilated my southern self. It was no different from what the converts to Christianity, the ones I'd thought were forever lost, had done. I didn't care.

I sheared my vowels short, then nasalized them. I knew it was working when new people stopped asking where I was from. Instead of Edward, I became "Eddie," which seemed more hip and urban. When I moved from the dorm into the fraternity house, I held a clothing sale, shedding my southern button-downs and penny loafers for a more "continental" look of Italian knits and—yes—white shoes. I had changed all the most basic elements of my identity—my voice, my appearance, my very name.

All my life I'd been trying to join a group, but at the ZBT house I was finding that except for the *wildes*—the rebels to whom I was naturally drawn and who had one by one dropped out of ZBT—my fraternity brothers were just too nice, too normal, as constraining to me as Marie Hull's magnolias had been. One day I simply packed my things and without telling anyone moved back into 30-E. When I called my parents, I could sense my father's fond illusions of future business contacts crashing at the other end of the line in Mississippi. My mother, herself never belonging, was perhaps even more disappointed.

"Do what you want. You always do anyway," she said.

ZBT, however, would not let me simply resign. Unless my parents kept paying a thousand dollars a year for food I wasn't eating and a room I had vacated, I would be expelled. As the letter from the ZBT executive secretary warned, "No young man can afford to have expulsion from his college fraternity on his lifetime record." My father was horrified, and even I was alarmed.

My mother began a protracted negotiation with the executive secretary, including a personal meeting with him when she and my father were in New York for the clothing market, but two months later I received official notice of my expulsion from the fraternity. It was the second Jewish organization I'd been thrown out of and I wasn't even out of my teens.

The next semester I moved off campus, where I continued my mutation into a northern Jew. I bought a poker table, the only furniture in my apartment, and around it sat street-smart northern Jews—fellow ZBT dropouts—who knew how the world worked. Klein had enviably staccato speech. Winston, who faithfully lost his allowance every month to Klein, possessed a black humor that matched my own. Richie was blessed with an easy smile, an eternal tan, and a knowledge, compounded daily, of what was hip.

I surrounded myself with them and their friends, hoping some of it would rub off and counteract a lifetime of being protected. I had grown up in a place where, if someone said something, you could pretty well believe them. In the world beyond, I was finding that this sensibility didn't apply. My father had said don't let anybody push you around, and the only way I knew to toughen up was to become someone else.

Classes were the least of my education. My friends and I

would leave at 1 A.M. on a school night for Jilly's, a Miami Beach nightclub whose back room was frequented by Frank Sinatra, though we never located the back room, much less entered it. We knew to arrive at jai alai for only the last three games of the night, when the good players drove up the odds, though not ever to our benefit. We took spur-of-the-moment midnight flights to the Bahamas, where forty minutes later we'd be gambling, James-Bond-like, at a casino with British croupiers. Arriving back in Miami at 4 A.M., we'd have plenty of time to make it to the beach, where we'd lie on our personal portable lounge chairs, glistening with DeepTan lotion with O SPF, each holding metal sun reflectors under our chins to maximize the rays.

Back in Mississippi, my friends were dancing the alligator and residing in trailers. Except for the fact that it was true, it seemed impossible that I had ever lived there.

The sixties arrived for me some time around 1968, and, since I'd been outside the mainstream for twenty years, I was ready for them. Back in Mississippi, Camp and Crell remained at their end of our generation's divide, while Ralph joined me on the other. My white shoes joined my wing tips in oblivion. My hair grew long and curly, I wore round wire-rim glasses, and my mother noted, uncomplimentarily, that I looked exactly like an immigrant. She despaired particularly at the frazzled foot-long tail of cloth that trailed behind my floor-dragging bell-bottom jeans and begged me to let her cut it off.

By that time I'd managed to search out and find, off campus, a Christian girlfriend despite the overwhelming preponderance of Jewish girls in my circle at school. Lynda had sun-streaked blonde hair, and though she was from New York, her voice was soft. She was a rebel, an artist, and an outcast, for me an irresistible combination. Her father had been the illustrator who created the Campbell's Kids, but he and Lynda's mother had recently died, and Lynda was suddenly exiled from her childhood home and living with her sister, who was in some secretive government agency and disapproved of me.

We visited Mississippi during the summers and at Christmas, and my friends there found Lynda as exotic as she found them. It was Lynda whom Granny pulled me away from after a Christmas Eve store dinner, telling me to stay with my own kind. After Miami, Jackson felt suffocating, primitive. Everything seemed small and everyone seemed slow.

In the summer of 1969 Lynda and I arrived home thin as refugees because of our macrobiotic diet. My mother, horrified, looked at my suitcase, which was full, not of clothes, but of brown rice. I wouldn't eat her stuffed cabbage, her potato latkes, or her incomparable kreplach, so she determinedly went through my macrobiotic cookbook and made me elaborate rice and soy fritters to try to fatten me up. Neither she nor my father commented on my new accent.

During those visits to Mississippi, I felt simultaneously like an impostor and an intruder. My newly engrafted northern identity was face-to-face with my recently shed southern self. Each time I came home, I felt that the distance travelled was as much through time as through space, into a past that stubbornly persisted despite all my efforts at eradication. Each time I returned to Miami, I felt liberation but also loss, as if I were suffering from self-imposed amnesia.

It had long been apparent that I was not travelling my mother's path to academic excellence. I had started college in 1966 with no idea of what career I might go into, and four years later I still didn't know. I'd considered majoring in English, since it appeared to be related to writing, but instead chose mass communications, which seemed to resemble an English major but didn't require the reading of any books. I made an esoteric three-minute film about the creation and end of the world, as dramatized by building blocks, but didn't receive any job offers. As a friend who was in the same major said to me, "This mass communications is easy, but what do you do with it?"

I had no idea either. After eighteen years on Brook Drive and four at the beach, I was utterly unprepared to do anything with my life. Everything had been theoretical in school, or perhaps I'd missed all the classes when they talked about jobs.

School was coming to an end. Klein, Winston, and Richie had long since dropped out, and the rest of my friends would, very soon, be graduating and returning home to New York. Home was where you went when you finished school, and though by now I felt northern, my transformation was not so complete as to provide me a past. My real past, Mississippi, seemed to belong to another person, someone I'd once known, then outgrown and forgotten.

In accordance with my escape plan, I'd left Mississippi with the intention of never returning, and my visits there had reinforced my determination. My telephone conversations with my mother were becoming increasingly uncomfortable.

"I hope you don't expect just to stay down there forever, doing nothing."

I hadn't framed it exactly like that in my mind, but what she said bore some resemblance to the amorphous cluster of thoughts that could loosely be termed "my plans."

"Because you can forget that right now, Edward Charles Cohen."

To stay out of Mississippi I had to find a job. I visited every television station in Miami, but they'd already said no to the hundreds of other students who'd preceded me by six months.

By the time I graduated, a semester late, in January 1971, the campus was full of strangers. The commune where I lived (a marker of the distance I'd travelled from Brook Drive) had collapsed, and the dramatic end of my three-year relationship with Lynda coincided almost exactly with the anticlimax of graduation. I felt utterly unmoored, as lost as the night in 30-E when my parents left.

I took the civil service exam. I didn't know what else to do.

An opening appeared for playground instructor, and sports seemed less inconceivable than returning to Mississippi. I interviewed for the position. The job entailed rounding up kids in the park, organizing a ball game, and supervising them. I'd be unsupervised, outside where I might meet a girl, and allowed to keep my long hair. This was 1971, and I was not alone in my priorities. Most importantly, I'd have a job.

The civil service position I most coveted was that of trash collector, specifically the branch of the service that collected fallen palm fronds. I'd seen those guys, shirtless, getting good rays, hair down their backs, rebelliously blue collar.

I dialed home. "I took the civil service exam, Ma."

After a long pause at the other end of the phone, she asked, finally, "How did you do?"

Actually, I had done very well, my first decent grade in—how many, ten?—years. It was amazing how the situation had concentrated my mind.

"You could make a good career with the government," she said guardedly, no doubt envisioning something maybe in the State Department. I had enough sense not to mention the trash collecting, at least not until I had locked down the position.

"Lots of security," my father noted encouragingly on the other line. He mentioned that Camp and Crell and Ralph were back from school, and I suppressed the feeling of how good it would be to see them.

The government moved at its usual rate, and many other college graduates as adrift as I were competing with me for the positions. By now, two months had elapsed since graduation.

One of my few business contacts managed a circus then wintering in Miami. From my increasingly desperate perspective, the circus seemed a not-unrealistic possibility— definitely exotic, with lots of travel, though a modest return on investment for the thousands of dollars my parents had sunk into my bachelor's degree. It would also, I knew, be a toughening experience, which I craved. I still felt, underneath my lacquered-on accent, like the same immigrant Mississippi Jewish hick dancing the polka-rock at the nightclub that first night in the big city.

On the drive out to meet the manager at the wintering ground outside Miami, I envisioned becoming involved with a beautiful trapeze artist, living in a colorful circus wagon, being a true bohemian. I waited for an hour, then two. The circus employees, whom I'd imagined might be genteel artistes, reminded me of the burly anti-Semitic rednecks I had been afraid of at the pool hall down the street from the store. One of them challenged my presence, and, when I invoked the manager's name, sullenly offered to show me around.

I didn't see any girls at all, much less lithe trapeze artists, and instead of little painted wagons there were tiny rusting trailers, where employees bedded down en masse. I passed cage after cage of dispirited animals wilting in the heat. My guide pointed to their soiled cages, and I realized what my career would be. He smiled, his first, and I saw he had no teeth.

* * *

April came, and I was still wintering in Miami. My long-graduated friends, whose prospects had once seemed as hopeless as mine, had jobs, jobs for which, remarkably, their majors had prepared them. I saw Lynda occasionally, as a friend. I went to a beach every day, not Miami Beach where once we lounged, our reflectors upraised in a salute of hedonistic unity, but to a small quiet inlet on Key Biscayne where I walked for hours by myself, hoping I'd see someone I knew. Days would go by without my speaking a word to another person.

Even so, I was determined to stay. I had struggled and planned since I was thirteen to pull free from the gravitational grip of Mississippi, and had briefly succeeded, but now I was in free fall. Going back—I disciplined myself not to say "going home"—seemed like a long plummet to a small place.

With the necessity of invention, I birthed another scheme. I had never painted a house, but after several days of canvassing businesses in the artsy Coconut Grove area, I managed to bid so low on a job that I got it, with the promise of more work if that assignment went well. I felt suddenly moored, part of the great machine of commerce, a tax-paying citizen of Miami with a valid reason to be there. I rented a giant spray rig from a paint store, along with drop cloths and ladders, and soon was two stories high, buffeted by intermittent winds. By the end of the first afternoon, I'd covered one side of the large building with burnt umber (my employer's choice) and moved around to the front. Here I had to be more careful to avoid painting the display windows, and I kept the spray nozzle aimed high.

When I came down for a break, I noticed that the shiny metallic-blue Porsche parked in front of the building looked as if a flock of hummingbirds had flown over it with burnt-umber diarrhea. I touched the car. The paint was as fast drying as the wizened painter at the shop had promised.

I scraped tentatively at anumber splotch with my fingernail, but it seemed to have bonded with the very metal.

I could tell that the car was beloved by its owner, who would be just the sort of person to make a big deal out of this. Thinking fast, I remembered a grocery store on the corner.

The steel wool easily removed the paint. Within thirty minutes I had scoured away every trace. The car was blue again, but a more muted blue, a troubled blue. I had no idea how much damage I had done, what it would take to fix it. Somewhere at the edge of my panic nibbled the fear that I was going to have to ask my father to clean up the mess.

The owner of the Porsche turned out to be my employer, the one who was going to get me other work, the custodian of my career. He was remarkably quiet for someone so enraged, although he did manage to get out that my pay would go toward meeting his insurance deductible. All that work—and days of work yet remaining—for which, at the end, there would be no pay.

Walking alone on the beach again, lost at age twenty-two, my resolve crumbling like a barricaded sand castle at high tide, I finally looked at my two choices with clarity. Yes, the South was conservative, constraining, and unglamorous, home to few Jews and no haven for rebels or artists. But neither was it a place where transients briefly lighted, then fled home, leaving no mark except upon me, the rear guard in a war no one else knew about. The South had its own solid identity, one that it wasn't afraid to claim, and that seemed important. Most of all, the South was by its nature welcoming, and a welcome was what I needed most.

With increasing excitement and also enormous relief, I managed to pack all my possessions—every wall-sized Indian bedspread, every Country Joe album, even a bentwood rocker—in my Mississippi-tagged car (it had always been the one clue I couldn't hide). As I drove onto the Sunshine State Parkway, the exit from Miami into the interstate netherworld, I looked through the rearview mirror at the city of strangers as it receded in the distance. As I picked up speed, I felt, unexpectedly, a surge of unalloyed joy. I *was* going home.

Epilogue

> A ship is safe in a harbor but that is not what a ship is for.
> Anonymous, from my mother's "Pearls of Pauline"

I lost part of my New York accent on the drive home, somewhere in Alabama when I couldn't resist the urge to pull over at a barbeque stand, and the rest wore off like a bubble-gum tattoo. Mississippi was slower, about the speed of life. By degrees I was reabsorbed. If I still didn't know who I was, at least I knew who I wasn't.

Somehow my mass communications degree and my writing came together, and I was hired as a writer at Mississippi ETV, where I embraced film projects that, not surprisingly, were about misfits and outcasts such as Walter Anderson, the artist who felt at home only when alone on an island.

ETV was my island, but I wasn't alone. There were writers, directors, and artists, many of whom, like me, had gone away and come back. Henry Kline, a southern Jew whose father had roomed with my father at Tulane, had gotten as far as New York before gravity and family drew him home. Together we made numerous programs, including a history of Hanukkah, which we exported to the New York PBS affiliate in a satisfying reversal of cultural influence.

My mother, like her parents, fought a long war with cancer. She never stopped sending out her "Pearls," even when she was too weak to get out and had to make each copy by hand. At the end, when most of her lungs were gone and she fought for every breath, the doctor offered to put her on a respirator while she underwent probably fruitless tests.

"Then you'll take me off?" she managed to get out. She'd had a long acquaintance with respirators from her hospital volunteer work.

"No," he said. "Once you're on it, we can't take you off." Panic flew across her face, something I'd never seen there.

"You mean I have to decide *now*?" He nodded. It took her no more than a moment to make her determination.

"Then I don't want it," she said, with what I thought was astonishing courage. And that, except for telling me she loved me, was the last thing she ever said.

I changed careers and became a lawyer, joining a large firm where I had my usual experience with groups— expulsion. It was as a lawyer that I had the sad duties of helping sell the store and later the house on Brook Drive.

Ann, Lolita, and Pearle died within a remarkably short time after my mother's death. Of the older generation, only the four Cohen men were left, and the Big House reconstituted itself yet again as my octogenarian father (the only one not night-blind) drove Lazar, Buddy, and Marvin to suppers at the Piccadilly Cafe. Then, one by one, they left Jackson to join their children. The 1995 Jackson phone book showed seven Cohens descended from Moise and Sam; the 1996, none.

Despite my old escape plan, my home state had exerted a far greater hold on me than I would have ever guessed possible. Thirty years after my first foray out, I left Mississippi a second time, for California, to write. My father was anchored in the South, but with my mother gone and now me, the old gambler went for the long shot. If the sheer size and speed of Los Angeles were a shock to me, for him the stun was as palpable as a sledgehammer blow. Panicked, he returned to Jackson, trying to regain his footing, but no one was there and he came back.

Here he talks about the store and, increasingly, the Big House. He calls Lazar on the other coast. He wonders if he should have sold Brook Drive, forgetting all its sad reminders. His manners, compared with those of the other residents of his retirement hotel, seem so southern and courtly as to date from another century. On the elevator he's determined to let ladies off first, as any southerner would, but no one understands and he gets in the way. More than once, Tiger has risen to defend his home state, even offering to step outside. I took him to temple, hoping he'd find a connection there, but his Jewishness, like mine, can't be found in a building.

In Los Angeles, everyone seems to be an immigrant, and no one is excluded or thought too different. Even though my provincial brand of Judaism is unremarkable in this informal climate, I still feel set apart from the many Jews around me by my other, southern half. Some call me "terminally polite," not a compliment, but I make no apologies. In this rootless city I treasure my history, and, this time, I know not to change. Out here, if you don't know who you are, you won't be that way for long. This time I've held onto my accent.

From the first day my Jewish self was suddenly full-immersion baptized into that southern world, I wanted to reconcile what couldn't be joined. I might not be comfortable on any one shore, but now I've learned the difference between discovering who I am and inventing it. Invention for me meant erasure, and whether it was my southern or my Jewish half that I hoped to lose, each time I tried, I got smaller.

I always knew that my Judaism went so deep I could never lose it, but it's taken two exiles to see how much of the South I carry with me. Back home there's gravity, and it holds you tight to the earth. I miss strangers waving on country roads and even city streets. I miss voices that cradle you. I miss people who remember my grandfather. Out here, when I hear a southern accent, I know that if I need help, that's who I'll ask.

It seems that a few generations in the South exert almost as much pull as an Old Testament of time, and I'm hard put to say where the southern leaves off and the Jewish begins. I may be a man without a country, but I carry two passports.

Acknowledgments

To Macy B. Hart, Executive Director of the Museum of the Southern Jewish Experience, and Hunter Cole at the University Press of Mississippi, for their continuing support over many years; to JoAnne Prichard who, with Hunter, first saw the possibility of this book; to my editor, Craig Gill, for his steady encouragement; to Carol Cox, for her lapidary copyediting; to my father, Leonard P. Cohen, my cousins Lazar Cohen, Buddy Cohen, Marvin Cohen, Gary Cohen, Roslyn Frank, Janice Knowles, and Marilyn Rothstein, and my aunt and uncle, Marcia and Louis Weltman, for sharing their recollections and for all our good years together.